The Infinite Money Glitch:

The Guide for Financial Freedom through Multi-family Real Estate

By
Adam Demchik & Mike Mannino

ISBN: 978-1-963502-94-7

Table of Contents

Legal Disclaimer:

The information provided in this book is for educational and informational purposes only. While the author has made every effort to ensure the accuracy and completeness of the content, they are not providing legal, accounting, tax, or investment advice.

Readers are advised to consult with their own qualified professionals, including but not limited to accountants, tax advisors, and attorneys, before making any financial or investment decisions based on the information presented in this book.

The strategies, techniques, and concepts discussed in this book, including but not limited to depreciation, 1031 exchanges, and tax benefits associated with holding multi-family properties, may have legal, tax, or financial implications that vary based on individual circumstances and jurisdictional requirements.

The author and publisher disclaim any liability or responsibility for any loss or damage resulting from reliance on the information provided in this book.

Readers should independently verify any information contained herein and seek professional advice tailored to their specific situation before implementing any strategies or making any investment decisions.

By reading this book, you acknowledge and agree that the author is not providing personalized financial, tax, or legal advice and that you are solely responsible for evaluating and determining the suitability of any strategies or recommendations for your own financial and investment objectives.

This document is for educational purposes only and does not constitute an offer to purchase or sell securitized real estate investments. Private Real Estate Investments are available to accredited investors and accredited entities only. Requirements for accreditation are defined in Rule 501 of Regulation D. Investors are required to self-certify their accreditation status and should consult a CPA or attorney if uncertain.

There are risks associated with investing in multi-family real estate, including, but not limited to, loss of entire investment principal, declining market values, tenant vacancies, and illiquidity. Potential cash flows, returns, and asset appreciation are not guaranteed and could be lower than anticipated. Past performance is not indicative of future returns.

Individual investor needs and objectives vary, and this document is not intended to indicate multi-family suitability for any particular investor. In addition, it should not be interpreted as tax or legal advice. Investors considering a multi-family investment should speak with their tax and legal advisors for advice and/or guidance regarding their individual financial situation.

Photos in this document are either original or open-sourced. They are for illustrative purposes only and do not represent current or future multi-family offerings.

About Us

Adam Demchik

Adam is a highly accomplished engineer, real estate investor, and entrepreneur with a career that spans two decades. Adam has several real estate related businesses including a private lending company and a multifamily investment company.

He has funded over 300 loans for real estate investors in the Metro Detroit area and has 300+ units under ownership.

With over a decade of multi-family experience, he currently has over $30,000,000 of real estate assets under management.

Mike Mannino II

Over the past 9 years, Mike has built a business that flipped over 90+ houses in Metro Detroit. He now resides in South Carolina while still operating his fix and flip company virtually.

Taking his construction and project management knowledge, he quickly scaled with Reciprocity Capital Group and currently owns over 100+ apartments.

He is the founder of multiple companies that generate over $1M per year in revenue and the owner of Real Estate Wealth Builders, an educational company that helps real estate investors quickly scale their real estate business.

Why Multi-family?

Our Story

When we got together to write this book, one thing that we really knew we wanted to convey was our "why." Our "why" for investing in the multi-family space. Without knowing why we were doing this, what drive would we ever have to succeed to the next level?

We both came from different moments in our lives when we realized the power of multi-family investing.

Different ages

Different backgrounds

Different careers

Different family lives

And you will too. Our "why" isn't going to be your "why," and our "aha" moments will be different than your "aha" moments.

You picked up this book for a reason. You might already have a "why," or you might know that you need to do something different, and you haven't found yours yet. We hope that this next section will give you some context of our "why" and our "aha" moments.

Mike Mannino II Perspective. We have one of the top flipping businesses in Michigan. From 2016 to 2023, our company has flipped 90+ houses, which is a great cash-producing business. I'm very blessed for where we are at and what we have accomplished.

But in 2020, after flipping 40+ houses, I realized something. The second I stop flipping houses, my income comes to a complete halt. I was hearing stories of people my age coming down with cancer, being diagnosed with a disease that prevented them from being able to work. I thought. "What if this happened to me? Where would I be financially? What money would be coming in?"

Or simply, what if I get burnt out of flipping houses? Because when you have 10+ house projects going on, spending $100,000+ per year trying to source discounted houses, managing contractors, and dealing with the unforeseen every day, it gets tiresome. So what If I wanted to take some time off?

Here's a photo of me with the first commercial real estate property I bought. Funny, come to think of it, this is actually the first property Adam and I bought together. It's a little 6-unit apartment building in Lapeer, Michigan. Originally, it was a home built in the 1880s, and then, at some point, it was converted into an apartment building.

I realized something about this property. After we bought it, we did the work of renovating it and increasing the rents to market. Every month, we got paid. Like, every month. From doing the major lift once, we get paid every month for as long as we hold the property.

This is an **AWESOME** feeling. Remember, I was used to only making money up to this point by flipping houses. I would get paid once, and then it was over.

I'll never forget the awesome feeling I had knowing I had money coming in without having to work for it.

After paying all of the expenses, property manager, and splits between the partners, I had about $600 left over per month going into my account. It's not life-changing money, but I was hooked!

With that money, I decided to buy a fun car. It had always been my dream since Transformers: The Movie came out with Shia LaBeouf back in 2007 to have Bumblebee. The Chevy Camaro was the coolest car in my eyes once that film came out. The car sat on my vision board for 13 years. Yes, for that long. Even having a successful fix and flip business for many years, I delayed the gratification.

Because I know that as much fun as this car is, it is a liability. Every month, the car depreciates, breaks down, and doesn't bring in any income. Yet, it takes money out of my pocket every month.

As much as I wanted this car, I just couldn't justify working for something that goes down in value. If I'm going to work for something, I want it to be appreciated over time and put me in a better position in life.

But with that $600 a month coming in that I didn't have to work for, I was able to justify spending a little money and finally getting my dream car.

"The only limit to your impact is your imagination and commitment."

– Tony Robbins.

Something funny about setting goals:

Someone I look up to is Jack Canfield, who wrote the famous book "Chicken Soup for the Soul." When he does goal-setting exercises, he always says, "End Goal or something better," leaving your end goal open to change for something better.

So, even after 13 years of seeing that car on my vision board, I ended up not buying the Camaro. But I believe I bought something better. I ended up getting a used 2017 Maserati Ghibli.

At first his sounds crazy, but the car was only $36,000 with 39,000 miles on it. The payment for the car is only $660 per month. Something that's fun and exotic for the same payment as a new Camaro. Pretty neat, huh?

So here's the breakdown:

$600 monthly rent - $660 car payment = $60. So now I only have to pay $60 for that car every month.

That's the power of buying an asset first (something that puts money in your pocket every month) to then pay for your liabilities (something that takes money out of your pocket every month).

My tenants basically paid for my fun car. I look at it as getting a free, fun car paid for by my tenants. It was that "aha moment."

What if we could buy 100 of these units? What would this look like?

On average, we look for properties that, after we renovate them and bring the rents up to market, yield about $200 profit per unit per month after paying all expenses.

100 units x $200 = $20,000 per month

Now that's some life-changing money. This would replace my highly active income from fixing and flipping houses, yet it would be a lot more passive.

Teaser: Just wait until I talk about the tax benefits of multifamily properties. Last year, I paid $0 in federal income taxes.

"The best investment on Earth is Earth."

– Louis Glickman.

Tornado Turned into Millions:

One of the great benefits of real estate is that you can insure the property in case of unforeseen events.

Imagine if you could insure a stock in case something happened to the company!

A friend of mine owns a 100+ unit apartment building in Ohio. The average rent there is about $850 per month per unit. Unexpectedly, a tornado came through and damaged all the buildings.

Thankfully, no one was seriously injured. While such a disaster is terrible, insurance came to the rescue. He was able to collect his monthly income from the insurance company to pay the mortgage and rebuild the buildings.

Now, instead of older 1980s units, he has newly built 2020s units renting for $1,500 per month per unit! That's an extra $650 per unit, and with 100 units, it totals $65,000 per month extra or $780,000 per year.

Later on, we'll discuss how multi-family properties are valued. This increase adds $10,000,000+ to the property's value.

So, despite the unfortunate event, my buddy made **$10M+** and an extra $780,000 per year. Suddenly, it doesn't sound like a disaster anymore.

What other investment can offer such resilience?

Adam Demchik's Perspective: At 8 years old, I knew I wanted to be an engineer, working in the automotive industry like my dad, who owned a small manufacturing company making components for cars. Exciting, right? For the next 15 years, I geared my life around becoming an automotive engineer.

In high school, I focused on getting good grades in math and science, and for college, I attended GMI Engineering and Management Institute. Six months before graduation, I was offered a full-time position as a quality assurance engineer at a company I had been interning at—**amazing!** I finished my degree during the day and then commuted one hour each way to work a split shift for the company that graciously hired me early.

Six months later, I was ready to graduate college early with a BS in Mechanical Engineering and a full-time job—except I was diagnosed with Hodgkin's disease less than a week after graduation. For those wondering, that's cancer. So I spent the next 6 months undergoing chemotherapy and radiation to have a clean bill of health for my wedding a month later. Quite a year.

Fast forward 10 years of working as an engineer, getting promoted several times to VP of Sales and Engineering, and starting a small business—I was at the top of my game. I had an amazing wife, three beautiful girls, and an incredible house, and I survived the Great Recession intact!

Then, I sold my little company and helped sell the company I was a VP at, all at the same time. Dang... I went from super entrepreneur to W2 employee really quick. No biggie. They gave me shares of stock and a $15,000 raise, plus a bonus plan!

But then the red tape started. Working for a small company and managing my own company turned into filling out purchase orders for the smallest office items and endless meetings with coworkers who seemed to think their entire job was sitting in meetings all day. It crushed my entrepreneurial spirit and made me miserable.

Then came a lot of travel and day trips to Korea—yes, Korea with a 14-hour flight from Detroit! Between my wife asking if I would ever focus on our family (what, 7 pm phone calls with China are a bad thing?), my pastor asking me to put effort into the church finance team, or my mom asking what happened to Mother's Day, I knew something had to change! I needed to move to something that I knew a little about, and that provided me the freedom to be home with my family while ensuring I could pay the bills for that amazing house I bought.

Hmmm.... what do I know about? Engineering, engineering, and the stock market—well, at least I knew what Apple stock was doing every day. Sounds like a plan! I quit my job and became a day trader overnight. I spent countless hours learning candlestick charts and why options were so powerful. But after about 6 months, I also learned that I had no control over the outcome of the companies I was buying or selling, nor did I appreciate the tax rates I was going to pay. And, as a day trader, if I wasn't buying or selling, I wasn't making any money. So I looked for something else I knew.

Well, I knew about houses since I lived in one, and my dad had some industrial space he rented, so I figured rentals wouldn't be too hard. There were those flipping shows on TV, and that looked fun!

So, in 2012, while I was still day trading, I got my real estate license and started reading books on real estate. Probably the most impactful were Rich Dad, Poor Dad, and the related books written by Robert Kiyosaki. I learned:

- What an asset is and why it puts money in your pocket
- Why and how the rich do not work for money
- Why the rich pay no taxes
- How the rich create generational wealth through real estate investing

Needless to say, I was hooked. But Rich Dad, Poor Dad didn't talk about flipping single-family homes, which is really sexy—*remember Mike above?* He talked about buying and holding assets (rentals) that put money into your pocket without having to show up to a W2 job every day, trade stocks, or work as a small business owner.

So after about 9 or 10 months of research, talking to brokers, investors, meetups, books, and analyzing properties with Excel spreadsheets (my personal favorite), I took the plunge and put a 48-unit apartment building in Holly, MI, under contract (we signed a purchase agreement).

(Grange Oaks Apartments in Holly, MI)

The biggest lesson learned here is that you make money when you buy the property. This property was clearly distressed, with 8 of the 48 units vacant and in need of major renovation. However, it had a good tenant base in a growing area of Michigan.

During inspection, we found what seemed like multiple issues at the time, but now they were all easily solvable. So, what did we do? We took the plunge and closed on the property. In fact, our family told us this was a bad idea. All the typical objections were brought up:

- Midnight no-heat calls

- Difficult tenants

- Evictions

- Rising bills

- Lawn care and snow removal

- Tornadoes

- Roof leaks

- Overflowing toilets

- Etc...

What I saw was an asset that produced monthly income (CASHFLOW) from Day 1 operations, an asset that would only increase in value, and something that would start a generational wealth machine for my family for years to come.

A week after we purchased, our rent collections were $17,000 for the first month. To be clear, that's not profit or cash flow, but getting a $17,000 shot into the bank account for something I didn't have to physically work on was a game changer.

From there on out, I got a quick education in operating apartments and what I could do to increase value through forced appreciation (more on this exciting topic later) and increasing rents through smart remodeling and unit turns.

Seeing the direct impact I could have on the income a property was generating and the value of the property, I quickly added more units to my portfolio in 2014. These purchases provided enough income for my family to live a great lifestyle from just 84 units.

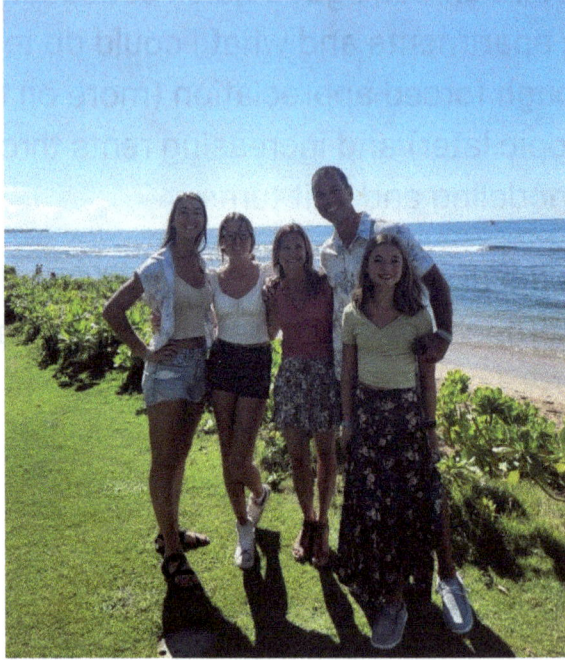

(Photo of the annual family Hawaii trip)

I spent the next few years improving operations and management of the properties, and in doing so, I doubled the value of all the properties I had purchased. This is one big reason multi-family real estate is so resistant to foreclosure. In just a few short years, I was able to:

- Double the value of our properties

- Achieve an LTV (loan-to-value ratio) on these properties of about 40% (which keeps our lenders happy)

- Increase the DSCR (debt service coverage ratio) to over 3! That means I could cover my mortgage payment 3 times every month with the profits I was making. For example, if my mortgage payment was $5,000.00 per month, I was bringing in $15,000.00 per month, allowing me more than enough cushion to cover my mortgage payment in case of unexpected issues.

Needless to say, I was hooked.

I saw the potential for multi-family investing to change the trajectory of my life and leave a legacy for my kids.

"The biggest risk is not taking any risk... In a world that is changing quickly, the only strategy that is guaranteed to fail is not taking risks."

– Mark Zuckerberg.

Why We Invest in Multifamily

We always several questions from other investors, business owners, or friends and family about why we are so EXCITED about investing in multifamily real estate. Below are a few questions we get and why we continue to invest in multifamily.

- Why multifamily versus other types of businesses?
- Why multifamily versus other classes of real estate?
- Why multifamily versus single-family homes?

Why multifamily versus other businesses?

There are many reasons people choose to invest in one business or another, some of them personal, and some of them are logical.

On the personal side, we invest in multi-family real estate to provide safe, clean, and nice apartments to our tenants. We all know landlords have a reputation...the slum lord. We don't operate our properties that way.

In fact, we strive to have the nicest apartment units based on the constraints of the market we operate in.

Do we have granite counters in a $ 700-per-month apartment? No, the property return wouldn't support granite counters at that lease rate in that market. But what we can do is have nicely painted units with new flooring, where needed, that are safe and comfortable. Take a look at our property in Redford, MI.

This is a small studio apartment, but wouldn't you agree that this is a really nice little place to live. The red fridge really makes it stand out!

The more logical reasons we invest in multifamily real estate are that it is a product that is "needed" in the market place and it has a known audience.

To put it simply, people always need a place to live and there is no need to sell them on a new product, service or invention.

That's not to say that some businesses don't become wildly successful or make millions of dollars for their investors and owners. I think of all the great businesses and products we use every day, from our cars to our social media. All were created and invented as new ideas and new businesses.

But I can't help but think of all the failed businesses from larger ones such as Blackberry (which had initial success but was quickly overtaken by the iPhone) to local restaurants I know that could not survive.

More simply put, real estate is physical. People need it and Amazon or Walmart are not going to replace the need for housing.

Why multi-family versus other classes of real estate?

1. **Meeting Housing Demand:** Multi-family apartments provide an essential housing option for a diverse range of demographics, including young professionals, families, empty nesters, and retirees.

2. **Affordable Housing Solutions:** Multi-family apartments offer a more affordable housing option compared to single-family homes, making them accessible to individuals and families with varying income levels.

3. **Economic Impact:** The development and operation of multi-family properties contribute significantly to the economy, generating jobs in construction, property management, maintenance, and related industries. Additionally, multi-family properties generate property tax revenue for local governments, which can support public services and infrastructure development.

4. **Community Building:** Multi-family properties often foster a sense of community among residents, offering shared amenities and common spaces where tenants can interact and socialize. This sense

of community can enhance residents' quality of life and contribute to the overall vibrancy of neighborhoods and urban areas.

5. **Adaptability to Market Conditions:** Multi-family properties tend to be more resilient to economic fluctuations compared to other real estate sectors. During economic downturns, demand for rental housing typically increases as individuals and families prioritize affordability and flexibility, making multi-family investments relatively stable and attractive to investors.

Why is Multi-family better than Single Family Homes?

Economy of Scale - With multiple units under one roof, operational expenses such as property maintenance, property management, utilities, and property taxes are consolidated, making them easier to manage and often more cost-effective.

For example, Adam and I, with our company Reciprocity Capital Group, own an 11-unit apartment building in Flushing, Michigan. There's a 3-unit house, and behind it are two beautiful 4-unit brick buildings built in the 1980s.

(Here's the property for reference)

We had to replace the roofs of the two buildings in the back that house a total of 8 units. Each roof cost us about $12,000 to replace, totaling $24,000 for the roofs of both buildings.

Doing some light math, that's about $3,000 per unit for the roof replacement.

If we had 8 houses that needed roof replacements, it would cost at least $8,000 per roof (and that price is extremely generous).

That roof replacement would have cost $64,000 for the 8 houses.

General maintenance

Multi-family:

For example, in our 44-unit property in Kentucky, we hired a part-time maintenance man who manages just our 44 units. With paint, electrical supplies, faucets, and plumbing materials all on the property, maintenance requests are handled quickly and cost-effectively.

When we first took over the property, I logged into our management software and saw a maintenance request from a tenant who was having an outlet problem. The request was submitted at 9:07 AM, which notified our maintenance guy, Andy. Andy was already at the property renovating another unit that was getting ready for market. He received the notification, walked over to the unit, identified the issue, went to the storage unit to grab the replacement part, and repaired the problem. This entire process took only an hour.

Single Family:

If this were a single-family house, the process would be much different. A maintenance request would come in, notifying the property manager. The property manager would need to coordinate with the tenant and the maintenance person for the best day and time to come out, which would likely be a few days later. Then, the maintenance person would drive to the house, diagnose the problem, drive to the nearest Home Depot or Lowe's to find and purchase the part, drive back to the house, and fix the issue. Hopefully, they grabbed the right part on the first trip, as house projects often require multiple trips to the store.

Once done, the maintenance person drives back to the office. This entire process for a quick fix could take half of the workday, costing the property owner much more than necessary.

See the Difference?

Fixing a small issue in a multi-family property is much more efficient and cost-effective compared to a single-family house, where the process is significantly more time-consuming.

Management - This one should be pretty quick to understand after my maintenance example.

Multi-family: You can have one single property with 100 units in one location. That's:

1 - Lawn to cut

1 - Property tax to pay

1 - Insurance policy

5 - Roofs

1 - LLC.

Single-family: Now imagine you have 100 houses. Do you know what that means?

100 - Lawns to cut

100 - Property taxes to pay

100 - Insurance policies (due at different times)

100 - Roofs

Potentially 100 LLC's

I'm getting the shakes just thinking about this 😨

Okay, so there are numerous other reasons like better financing options, resilience to market fluctuations, better management fees, and economies of scale...but there's one more I want to focus on. Forced appreciation.

> **Interested in the idea of adding multi-family to your portfolio?** Click here if you are on the digital version or enter the website link below to fill out a short questionnaire and book a 1-on-1 call with Mike and Adam. https://www.reciprocitycg.com/start-investing

Appreciation of Multifamily vs Single Family:

Multi-family:

In the next chapters of this book, we will talk more about and share real examples of real deals we have done and how we were able to force the appreciation of the property. Multi-family real estate is valued like a business. Its value is based on the net cash flow the property produces. So, the more the property makes at the end of the day, the more it's worth—pretty simple.

This is really beneficial for us real estate investors because we can mathematically estimate the future value of our properties by increasing the income and decreasing the expenses. For now, just know that if we **increase rents** and **decrease** expenses, the property's value goes up.

Single Family:

Houses, with which more people are familiar, are valued based on comparables or comps in the area of similar properties that are sold.

So, let's say there is a neighborhood of all 1,000-square-foot, 3-bed, 2-bath houses. If your neighbor to the left sold for $100,000 and your neighbor to the right sold for $100,000, guess what your house is going to be worth? Pretty close to that $100,000 number.

Even if you rented out the property for $1 per month or $1,000,000 per month, the property value of single-family residences wouldn't change because its value is not based on rent. It's based on what your neighbors sold for.

And that's why single-family isn't great for investors and businesses. There's no reward or upside for the owner increasing the income and decreasing expenses like there is on a business or multifamily property.

Multi-family is Recession Resistant:

In fact, during the 2008 financial crisis, which was one of the worst in our lifetime, only 0.8% of Fannie Mae and 0.2% of Freddie Mac agency loans went to foreclosure. That means less than 1% of apartment buildings with loans went into foreclosure. What a safe investment! During the peak of the financial crisis, less than 1% went back to banks.

Figure 2: Historical Agency Delinquency Rates

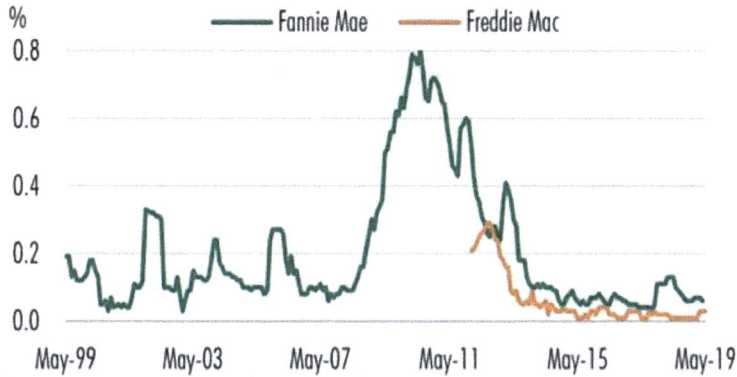

Source: CBRE Research, Fannie Mae (through April 2019), Freddie Mac (through May).

(Source: https://www.globest.com/2019/06/28/as-talk-about-gses-overhaul-swirls-multifamily-makes-a-good-case/?slreturn=20240408093149)

Our experience in the multifamily space has shown us the importance of two key factors that prevent the potential foreclosure of properties.

1.) Location

The most important takeaway from this is making sure you buy apartments in locations that have most or all of the following characteristics:

- Increasing population

- Good schools

- Job growth

- New or stable building in the area

- Favorable landlord-tenant laws (for when you have to evict tenants)

- And Starbucks... so you can get coffee when you visit your property! Just kidding! However, Starbucks, Chick-Fil-A, Whole Foods, and other companies put a lot of effort into selecting growing areas, so why not follow them?

2.) Management

In fact, the vast majority of apartment foreclosures are self-inflicted by poor ownership and management. It's the exact opposite of the way Adam was managing his apartments. We look to stabilize and optimize operations by reducing expenses and keeping rent in line with the market.

So, Adam wasn't an instant millionaire or a flipping king making a TV show, but he did accomplish his goals through multi-family investing. In fact, he knew that more millionaires are made through real estate than any other business in the world.

What Happened During the Great Recession?

Simply put, real estate is a long game. One of our mentors, Rod Khleif, said: "Real Estate is not a get-rich-quick, but a way to get extremely wealthy over time."

If you zoom out even over a short 50-year period, you can see that the cash flow from rents is extremely steady and consistent.

Check out this chart showing the monthly cost of buying vs. renting in America. The blue line indicates the monthly mortgage payment. You can see that over 50 years, it has trended upward. However, there are a lot more peaks and valleys.

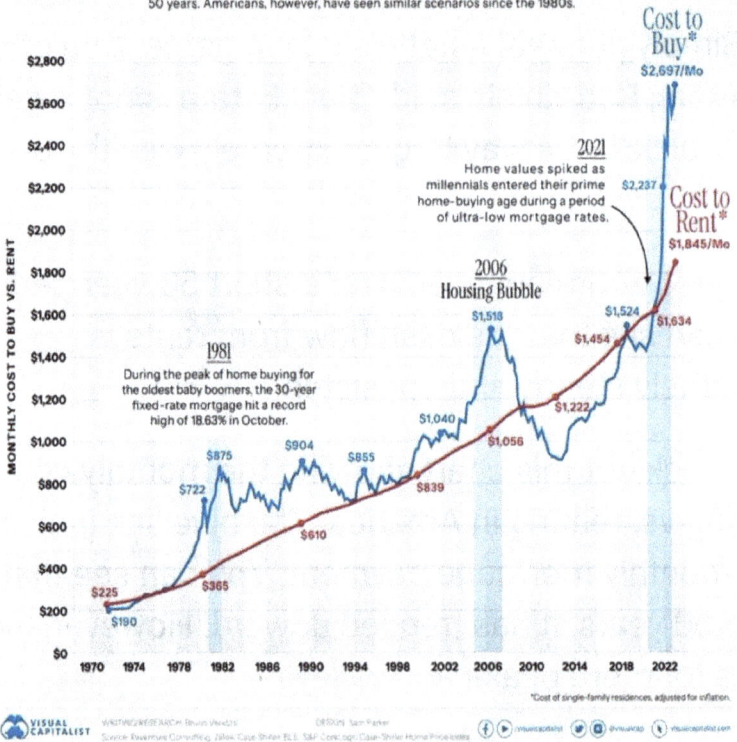

Buying vs. Renting ◇ in America

With home prices and mortgage rates both rising, the U.S. has witnessed the biggest numerical gap in cost between owning a home and renting in over 50 years. Americans, however, have seen similar scenarios since the 1980s.

Cost to Buy*
$2,697/Mo

2021
Home values spiked as millennials entered their prime home-buying age during a period of ultra-low mortgage rates.
$2,237

Cost to Rent*
$1,845/Mo

2006
Housing Bubble
$1,518

$1,524 $1,634

$1,454

1981
During the peak of home buying for the oldest baby boomers, the 30-year fixed-rate mortgage hit a record high of 18.63% in October.

$1,040 $1,222

$904 $1,056

$875 $855

$722 $839

$610

$365

$225

$190

MONTHLY COST TO BUY VS. RENT

*Cost of single-family residences, adjusted for inflation.

Look at the red line for the cost to rent. It's still very similar, constantly trending upward over the past 50 years, but it's a lot more stable and predictable. Even during the 2008 financial crisis, one of the worst

THE INFINITE MONEY GLITCH

crashes in financial history, rents remained steady while the cost of a mortgage drastically changed.

At the peak of 2006, the cost of a mortgage was about $1,518, and it bottomed out around 2012 at about $900 per month, marking about a 40% drop over a 6-year period. On the other hand, looking at the red line and considering the same time frame, rents peaked out at $1,056 in 2006 and actually grew to $1,222 by the time mortgage prices bottomed out in 2012.

What a massive difference, right?

It's reassuring to see that even in the worst financial crises in history, rents remain strong, predictable, and generally appreciated. Multifamily real estate is truly a very unique asset class like no other.

Now, imagine if you could go back to the 1970s and buy a multi-family property. Looking at the chart, you could charge $225 per month to rent the property out. Now, 50 years later, those same units would rent for $1,845 a month! That's over an 800% gain in rents.

Oh yeah. Your tenants would have also paid off the property for you 20 years ago if you had a traditional 30-year mortgage.

Mind-blowing 🤯

We hope that this last section has helped you develop an understanding of the massive benefits of multi-family investing, and we hope you can see "why" this investment is such a great way to fund your "why".

"90% of all millionaires become so through owning real estate."

- Andrew Carnegie

How is Multi-family Valued?

It would be hard to get into explaining our business plan and the **Infinite Money Glitch** without defining a few things first.

In this section, we're going to dive deep into the process of determining the value of multi-family properties and some of the terms used when looking to purchase a multi-family property.

As you may have picked up from our stories above, there are a few complicated-sounding but very simple terms in multi-family real estate. Hopefully, they didn't scare you off, because after reading this section, you should have a good idea of what these terms mean and why they are important to remember.

Net Operating Income (NOI)

Simply put, multi-family properties are valued by what the property makes after paying all of its expenses.

This is called the <u>Net Operating Income</u> or NOI for short.

The total income generated by a property minus the operating expenses, excluding debt service and income taxes.

NOI = Total Gross Income – Operating Expenses

Here is a screenshot of one of the calculators we use for underwriting a multifamily property. Now don't get freaked out when you first see this. There's a lot of information, but we are going to break it down together.

	2. My Version	
Asking Price	$900,000	
Purchase	$900,000	
# Units	16	
Price Per Unit	$56,250	
Down payment %	25%	
Down payment $	$225,000	
Interest Only (in months)	0	
Loan Balance	$675,000	
Repairs	$125,000	
Operating Reserves	$36,000	
Estimated closing costs	$44,507	
Total Acquisition Cost	**$1,105,507**	

Income		
Average Monthly Rent	$987	
Gross Potential Rent	**$189,504**	
- Vacancy	($9,475)	5.00%
- Concessions, Loss to Lease, Bad Deb	($4,738)	2.50%
Gross Potential Income	$175,291	
Other Income		
Effective Gross Income	**$175,291**	

Expenses		
Advertising	$0	0.00%
Contract Services	$10,500	5.99%
Gas & Electric	$1,500	0.86%
General/Admin	$0	0.00%
Insurance	$13,000	7.42%
Legal	$2,500	1.43%
Real Estate Taxes	$7,000	3.99%
Trash Removal	$3,000	1.71%
Management Fee	$19,282	11.00%
Payroll	$0	0.00%
Repairs and Maintenance	$6,000	3.42%
Turnover	$0	0.00%
Water and Sewer	$0	0.00%
Deposit to Replacement Reserve	$4,000	2.28%
Total Expenses (Added)	**$66,782**	**38.10%**
Total Expenses (Manual Override)	**$66,782**	**38.10%**
To Manually Override the Expenses to use %		
the dollar summary must be $0 on line 43		
Total Expenses	**$66,782**	**38.10%**
Net Operating Income (NOI)	**$108,509**	

We take all of our Effective Gross Income of $175,291 and subtract all of the expenses to run the property of $66,782, which leaves us with $108,509 in Net Operating Income. That's how much we take home after a year of running the property if we own it without a mortgage.

Cap Rate (Capitalization Rate)

It is the ratio of a property's net operating income to its purchase price. CAP Rate = NOI / Purchase Price

It helps investors assess the potential return on investment.

Example: If you owned a property in cash, what would your return on Investment be?

$108,509 Net Operating Income (NOI)

$1,000,000 Property Purchase Price

=

.108 or a 10.8% Return.

That's your Cap Rate.

The property was purchased at a "10.8 Cap."

If you purchased this property for $1,000,000 with no mortgage and earn $108,509 in Net Operating Income (NOI), you are receiving a 10.8% return on your money.

It's a simple equation, but it takes some practice to get used to running these numbers.

I get asked all the time, *"What is a good cap rate"* It depends on the area. In Flint, Michigan, it might be 15%, and in Miami, Florida, maybe 4%. It depends on the location, asset class, age, and the going cap rate in the market.

Okay, so now you have the idea. We are going to go over a real example in the next chapter

"Opportunities don't happen, you create them."

– Chris Grosser.

Cashflow

The amount of cash generated by a property after deducting operating expenses and debt service is known as cash flow.

Cash flow = NOI − (Capital Expenses + mortgage payments)

This is what we as investors take as profit.

This is what makes it back to your bank account every month.

Debt Service

Debt service is simply a fancy word for what is commonly called a mortgage payment. This is the amount of money you pay to the bank every month. It is sometimes called a "note" payment as well.

The Debt Service payment is calculated when you get a loan from the bank and is based on a couple factors:

1. <u>Interest Rate</u> − The rate of interest you would pay on an amount owed to somebody

2. <u>Amortization length</u> – The number of years the repayment of the loan is for.

You maybe familiar with the terms, but the definitions are above just in case you need a refresher.

Interest Rate

Obviously, the higher the interest rate is, the higher the payment will be. For example payments are calculated as such:

Loan amount x interest rate = Interest Payment

So it looks like this

$1,000,000 (loan amount) x 5% (annual interest rate) = $50,000 (annual interest payment)

For every 1% the interest rate goes up, and the payment would go up by $10,000. That makes shopping for the rate important! Talking to multiple banks and having relationships with mortgage brokers is critical for this.

Amortization length

The second part of the debt service payment calculation is the amortization length. This is the length at which the repayment of the original loan will be scheduled for. Typical amortization lengths in multifamily are 20- 30 years.

Being that there is a huge range of amortization length, our payment will vary greatly depending on the number of years of amortization length. To easily calculate this we would recommend an online mortgage payment calculator such as mycalculators.com.

So jumping back to our $1,000,000 loan example, the amortization length affects the payments as follows assuming a 5% interest rate:

20 Year Amortization - $6,599.56 (Principal and interest)

30 Year Amortization - $5,368.22 (Principal and interest)

Depending on your investment strategy, paying off the loan sooner with a 20-year amortization may be advantageous, but there is one other factor that is important in multi-family investing that might make you consider or even prefer a 30-year amortization. That's the DSCR ratio and that is where we are heading next.

Debt Service Coverage Ratio

Ok, don't close the book yet, I promise this is super simple yet very important. I know that Debt Service Coverage Ratio sounds awfully scary, so let's shorten it to the more common reference of DSCR.

Simply put, the DSCR is the ratio of NOI to the amount of your mortgage payments. So to put in in an equation:

DSCR = NOI / Total annual mortgage payment

Typically, many banks are going to require that the DSCR ratio, must be greater than 1.25, which means that you can pay your mortgage payment plus have an extra 25% of the mortgage payment to cover any issues.

Appreciation

Appreciation is simply the amount of value a property will gain over time. In multi-family investing, there are two types of appreciation:

1.) Forced Appreciation
2.) Natural Appreciation

Let's start with the easy one. <u>Natural appreciation</u>. This is just the simple increase in value over time due to inflation of materials, labor and the devaluing of the US dollar.

While these are typically small increases, they add up over time.

<u>Forced appreciation</u> as we alluded to in the previous chapter is the ability to increase the value of the property by increasing the NOI.

Remember, Multi-family is valued based on the amount of NOI a property generates each year. So the higher you can drive the NOI, the higher the value of the property.

If you look back at the section on NOI, it can be increased by either increasing income (rent) or decreasing expenses. This means that for every dollar you raise rent or conversely every dollar you save in expenses, you are increasing the value of the property!

Amazing, right?

Adam's Perspective:

Remember that property in Holly I mentioned earlier? One of the biggest gaps we had in the expenses was the property tax amount. We were still paying property taxes on a property valued much higher than what we actually paid.

Thankfully, there is a process to fight your property taxes in Michigan, but it sounded hard. Turns out, it wasn't! This was one of the easiest and biggest increases in the value of the property I could have accomplished.

When we purchased the property, the property taxes were approximately $27,000 per year! That actually isn't that bad on a property that size, but since I paid only $920,000 for the property, we were definitely overtaxed. I hired a consultant who did 95% of the work for a small fee, plus the costs of an appraisal to present our tax appeal to the tax tribunal board.

After all was said and done, my property taxes were reduced by $9,000 per year! But that's not all. Do you remember the formula above? My NOI immediately increased by $9,000, which, at a 7-cap rate, increased the value of our property by $128,000! That's right, I generated a six-figure increase overnight with a small investment of time and money! Multifamily is powerful.

Other expenses that can be easily reduced are contract services such as lawn maintenance, snow removal, pest control, and common area cleaning. These are small changes with huge impact.

Take, for example, the 11-unit in Flushing, MI we own. We saved $40 per month on hallway cleaning. You might be thinking, big deal, that's $480 per year! Barely enough for a couple of nice steak dinners. But when we apply a cap rate to that $480 per year savings, we get an increased value of almost $7,000.

What? We made $7,000 in instant equity, plus we get a few nice steak dinners a year? Sign me up.

The same can be done with increasing rents. Next, we are going to share a real-life example of our 1019 Cypress property and how we doubled the value of our property through rent increases!

Real Example: 1019 Cypress

Mike's Perspective: So, when talking about the power of cash flow and forcing appreciation, I want to give you a real example of a 16-unit multi-family property we purchased in North Carolina in August of 2022.

We will slowly walk through the story of this property and use the terms and fundamentals above to give you a good idea of how they work in a real-life example.

1019 Cypress

I'm going to let you in on a secret. But If I tell you, you can't tell anyone, okay?

Pinky promise?

...

This 1019 Cypress is my favorite building we own.

Yes. I said it.

I know they are like your kids, and you aren't supposed to pick favorites. But look at this place. 16,000 square feet of brick with beautiful columns sitting on 2 acres surrounded by trees, higher-end homes, and the high school on the same street.

1019 Cypress

Each unit is 1,050 Square feet, featuring 2 beds and 1.5 baths, hardwood floors, and in-unit washer and dryer hookups.

This is Mike Mannino II's retirement plan right here!

Oh, I almost forgot to mention. *$5 margaritas within a 10-minute walking distance.*

Umm.. Yeah, sign me up!

Okay, so here is where we get a little nerdy and start diving into the numbers. But you have done an **amazing job so far**. So I know you got this!

We purchased this beautifully magnificent property for $900,000.

INCOME		
Average Monthly Rent	$689	
Gross Potential Income	$132,288	
- Vacancy	($5,000)	3.78%
- Concessions, Loss to Lease, Bad Debt	$0	0.00%
Effective Gross Income	$127,288	
Other Income	$0	
Total Net Income	**$127,288**	

The day we purchased it, our average rents were $689 per month for 16 units. Some were $650 and others were $700, so the blend of all of them came out to $689.

$689 X 16 Units = $11,024 in gross monthly income

X 12 Months in a year

= $132,288 in annual Gross Potential Income

Pretty simple so far.

Then we remove vacancy. Since this property only charged about $700 a month for rent in this amazing area, it was ALWAYS full. People very rarely moved out because it was under market rent. So if you left, anywhere else you move to would be higher rent.

We remove the $5,000 per year in vacancy, leaving us with $127,288 in Total Net Income this property brought in annually.

Now we are going to subtract from the expenses listed below.

EXPENSES		
Advertising	$0	0.00%
Contract Services	$5,464	4.29%
Gas & Electric	$1,162	0.91%
General/Admin	$0	0.00%
Insurance	$3,496	2.75%
Legal	$1,000	0.79%
Real Estate Taxes	$10,000	7.86%
Trash Removal	$2,064	1.62%
Management Fee	$14,000	11.0 [1]
Payroll	$0	0.00%
Repairs and Maintenance	$9,600	7.54%
Turnover	$4,000	3.14%
Water and Sewer	$0	0.00%
Deposit to Replacement Reserve	$4,000	3.14%
Total Expenses (Added)	**$54,786**	**43.04%**
Total Expenses	**$54,786**	**43.04%**
Net Operating Income (NOI)	**$72,502**	

When we purchased the property, we estimated our expenses would be $54,786 per year.

Now we subtract our $127,288 in Total Net Income

Total Expenses $54,786

= $72,502 in Net Operating Income

Remember what that means?

If we owned it free and clear without a mortgage and paid cash for the property, We would make $72,502 per year. Pretty great, right?

Summary	
Debt Service	$57,100
Interest Rate	5.80%
Amortization (Years)	20
Cash flow after debt service	$15,402
Cap Rate (NOI/Sales Price)	8.06%
Debt Coverage Ratio	1.27

Property Value Per Cap Rate	
6.0%	$1,208,367
6.5%	$1,115,415
7.0%	$1,035,743
7.5%	$966,693

Now, let us look at the summary.

This is going to include our mortgage information.

When we purchased this property, we put 25% down and borrowed 75% of the purchase price from the bank.

Our mortgage payment for the year is $57,100. This is the last expense we need to pay.

So, we are going to subtract that from Net Operating Income (NOI)

$72,502 (NOI) - $57,100 (Debt Service) = $15,402

$15,402 is what's left after paying ALL of our expenses and mortgage. That's what we get to take home every year.

Not as exciting now, is it? Haha

But remember, real estate is a long-term investment, and rents typically increase over time. As the saying goes: *"The best time to plant a tree was 20 years ago. The 2nd best time is today."*

The best time to buy real estate was in 1970; the 2nd best time is today.

So going back to the numbers, remember this is how multifamily is valued, based off of the Net Operating Income and the going market Cap rate.

In this market, the going Cap rate is 7%. That means people are willing to get a 7% return on their investment if they own the property free and clear. Which comes out to that **$1,035,743** number.

That's the true value of the property the day we purchased it. So, on day one, we had about $100,000 in equity buying the property correctly. 🤲

When looking at an investment property, you want to see what the future value of the property is because this is where your margin or profit lies.

Remember I said that people never moved out of this property because the rents were way below market value? Well, this is what we look for. Something where we can force the appreciation and increase cash flow and increase the value of the property.

Where are we now?

Well, after purchasing this property, we had to fix some deferred maintenance.

- Parking lot needed to be re-seal coated
- HVACs were not working
- Trees had to be cut and trimmed
- We installed gutter guards
- Fixed broken and sunken concrete
- Small foundation repairs
- Invested money back into the cosmetics of the units as well

Within 18 months of purchasing the property, we invested $125,000 into the repairs of the property or what is called the Capital Expenditure (CapEx). **Now, our total investment into the property = $1,025,000.**

INCOME		
Average Monthly Rent	$987	
Gross Potential Income	$189,504	
- Vacancy	($9,475)	5.00%
- Concessions, Loss to Lease, Bad Debt	($4,738)	2.50%
Effective Gross Income	$175,291	
Other Income	$0	
Total Net Income	**$175,291**	

We increased the rents to closer to market rents while making improvements to the property. Bringing the current tenants to $925 per month and new leases to $1,050 per month.

Now, our average monthly rent is $987, a significant increase from the $689 per month previously, huh?

This is about a 40% increase in monthly rent.

Increasing our Total Net Income to $175,291 per year.

So now we are going to subtract our expenses again.

EXPENSES		Per Unit	
Advertising	$0	$0	0.00%
Contract Services	$11,623	$726	6.63%
Gas & Electric	$1,187	$74	0.68%
General/Admin	$0	$0	0.00%
Insurance	$6,863	$429	3.92%
Legal	$517	$32	0.30%
Real Estate Taxes	$6,900	$431	3.94%
Trash Removal	$2,824	$177	1.61%
Management Fee	$16,653	$1,041	9.50%
Payroll	$0	$0	0.00%
Repairs and Maintenance	$5,187	$324	2.96%
Turnover	$0	$0	0.00%
Water and Sewer	$0	$0	0.00%
Deposit to Replacement Reserve	$0	$0	0.00%
Total Expenses (Added)	$51,755	$3,235	29.52%
Total Expenses	$51,755		29.52%
Net Operating Income (NOI)	$123,537		

Total expenses turned out to be $51,755

$175,291 Total Net Income - $51,755 Total Expenses = **$123,537 Net Operating Income (NOI)**

Wait a minute.

Mike, are you telling me if this property was owned free and clear, this property would net you **$123,537 per year?!**

Yes, that's exactly what I'm saying.

A significant increase from the previous $72,000 NOI last year, huh?

Okay, we are almost done! And it's now getting exciting. 😆

Summary	
Debt Service	$57,100
Interest Rate	5.80%
Amortization (Years)	20
Cash flow after debt service	$66,416
Cap Rate (NOI/Sales Price)	13.72%
Debt Coverage Ratio	2.16

Remember, we still have a mortgage on the property, so let's subtract that from the Net Operating Income (NOI):

$123,537 (NOI) - $57,100 (Debt Service) = $66,437

$66,437 is what we get to take home every year. Isn't this a little more exciting than the $15,000 we were making last year?

That's **$5,536 per month** in pure profit. That's better than the average salary in America right now, working full-time, 40 hours per week. This is with one property that is professionally managed and now fully updated.

P.S. I realize that the calculator came up with $66,416 in cash flow, and our manual math came up with $66,437. The calculator missed $21 somewhere. That's why you have to double-check the calculator's work sometimes 😄

Okay, this is why multifamily is significantly better than single family. Remember when we talked about forced appreciation? Well, the property is still valued at a 7% cap rate, but our Net Operating Income has significantly gone up.

What's the new value?

Market Cap Rate And Value	
Market Cap Rate	7.00%
Fair Market Value (Based on NOI)	$1,764,517

Let's go do quick math on this again. **Drum roll, please!** 👺 👺 👺

$123,537 / .07 = $1,764,814!

(*Again, the calculator is slightly off, haha.*)

Wow. A huge difference.

Remember our total investment into this property is $1,025,000.

Let's see how much we have now forced the appreciation.

New Current Value $1,764,814 - $1,025,000 Total Investment = $739,814 increase due to forced appreciation!

So, we have forced the new appreciation of the property to over $700,000 in value added within 18 months.

Mind blown again?

So, if we decide at any point, we can sell the property and walk away with **$700,000 in profit**.

"The secret of success is to do the common thing uncommonly well."

— John D. Rockefeller Jr.

The Infinite Money Glitch

So you made it through our "Why" and "Aha" moments. Hopefully, you know what your "why" is at this point, and hopefully, these first few sections of this book have seen your "Aha" moment. If, for some crazy reason, you haven't yet, that's okay. Keep reading, because now we are getting to the exciting part!

Let's take a moment and say congratulations!

You made it through all the terms and fundamentals of multi-family investments, which is the most difficult part to grasp. We tried our best to break it down and make it fun 😄.

Now, this section is the best part of the book!

It's <u>so important</u> that we titled the whole book around this investing strategy. This is what really ties everything we have been talking about together.

Maybe this is your "Aha" moment, and you are ready to jump into multi-family investing.

Maybe you read the next section and think:

"Can't be done!

How can anybody do this?"

But we can promise you that anybody can do this.

Even you!

We don't have a fancy degree or any kind of schooling in real estate, and we are here to tell you that what we are about to show you can be done.

You might also have a bunch of objections like:

- This can't be legal
- I don't have the money to do this
- I don't have the time to do this
- I don't know the right people
- I'm not from the right background

We would encourage you to stay the course and finish the book. That's the first step.

Dream Big

What if we told you there was a way that you could have an INFINITE supply of money?

infinite 1 of 2 adjective

in·fi·nite (ˈin-fə-nət ◀)

Synonyms of *infinite* >

1   : extending indefinitely : ENDLESS
     infinite space

2   : immeasurably or inconceivably great or extensive : INEXHAUSTIBLE
     infinite patience

3   : subject to no limitation or external determination

How would that change your life?

How would that change your family's life?

I'm gonna go out on a limb here and say that you are by now, pretty interested in having an infinite supply of money.

The Infinite Money Glitch

I know, fancy title that sounds really mysterious and complicated. Like some type of computer program that one must master or some secret code that you must know.

But we are here to tell you the Infinite Money Glitch is real...

...And available to you and your family

...regardless of where you are in life

...and we've implemented it several times.

This chapter will explain what it is, and the rest of the book will explain how to find it.

The best explanation for the infinite money glitch is a funny term that is used in real estate investing circles... "mail-box money!"

I know it sounds funny, like is there a mailbox made out of money? But it's the concept that you own something that just magically drops money into your mailbox every month.

Now, think of that money showing up in your mailbox every month or quarter, but you don't have any of your money invested.

So, in other words, what if you could get a return on your investment in real estate, but not have anything invested?

The infinite money glitch is simply that. It's receiving money in your mailbox or, nowadays, more likely, your bank account via wire.

But the main caveat is you have ZERO capital invested.

Yes, it's mailbox money deposited into your bank account without any of your capital tied up.

The strategy is simple to explain but a little harder to implement...

To put the **"Infinite Money Glitch"** in more practical terms, it follows this process:

1.) Purchase a multi-family property using a bank loan and a cash down payment from investors or your own funds.

2.) Increase the value of the property. Force appreciation through rent increases or expense decreases (remember this increases the NOI which increases the value of the property)

3.) Refinance the property and receive all your original investment back.

4.) Keep the property cash flow intact for infinite returns.

For a real example, let's go back to our 1019 Cypress property to see how this plays out in real life on a real deal.

So, when increasing the property value this much. With over $1,000,000 in equity in the property, we have a lot of options. (remember, we only borrowed $680,000 from the bank)

We can keep this property as is, sell it for a check, or even go back to the bank and get our money back.

Yes, you read that right.

Since we have forced the appreciation so much, we can go back to our bank and show them.

"Hey, we are great operators. We have increased income, repaired the property, and decreased expenses. We would like to refinance this property off the new current value".

That's exactly what we did.

As you will read in our **Investment Strategy and Business Plan**, we will explain our thesis in more detail.

After going back to the bank, they agreed we did a phenomenal job. The banker even said he had never seen anyone do what we did as fast in the over 500 loans he had originated.

Refinance Time:

This is what the deal looks like now: We did a cash-out refinance and got a new loan for $1,100,000, replacing our old loan of $680,000. (Oh yeah, the bank's appraisal came in at $1,725,000 even.)

$1,100,000 new loan - $680,000 old loan = **$420,000 back to our investors**.

We successfully went to the bank and got all of our money and investors' money back from the bank, while still owning the property. (And still leaving $625,000 of equity in the deal... With only having less than 65% leverage in the property. *We are conservative and want to make sure we are never over-leveraged.*)

So now, we and our investors own this property with none of our own money, just the bank's money.

We now have $420,000 back to our investors. This is also non-taxable because it's debt. (More on this in the **Depreciation: Tax Benefits** section)

Refinance Summary:

Summary	
Debt Service	$81,723
Interest Rate	6.75%
Amortization (Years)	30
Cash flow after debt service	$41,813
Cap Rate (NOI/Sales Price)	13.73%
Debt Coverage Ratio	1.51

Property Value Per Cap Rate	
6.0%	$2,058,942
6.5%	$1,900,562
7.0%	$1,764,807
7.5%	$1,647,154

Now that we have refinanced the property, our new annual mortgage payment is $81,723, which leaves us with about $41,813 left in annual cash flow.

Or about $3,484 per month with $0 of our own money into the deal, creating an infinite return.

That's the Infinite Money Glitch

Wait, what?! Let's zoom out.

Within 18 months of purchasing the property, we were able to increase the rents, fix up the property, and refinance all of our money out, creating $700,000 in equity and $41,813 in annual income.

On one single transaction.

Are you as excited as I am?!

Because if not, you can stop reading right now.

Next chapter, we are going to talk about the wealth appreciation that comes along with owning multifamily and why we chose not to sell 1019 Cypress.

Interested in the idea of creating cash flow? Click here if you are on the digital version, or enter the website link below to fill out a short questionnaire and book a 1-on-1 call with Mike and Adam. https://www.reciprocitycg.com/start-investing

---

Free Goodwill

Would you help someone you've never met before? And it doesn't cost you any money.

If you have found this book valuable so far, would you please take one minute of your time and leave us an honest review of the book and the information shared?

Your feedback is incredibly valuable to us and to others. It doesn't cost you anything and typically takes less than 60 seconds.

Your review will:

...help one more person get out of the rat race.

...help one more person to support his or her family.

...help one more life change for the better.

To make that happen... all you have to do is leave a review on Amazon. It takes less than a minute.

Here's the next step:

Head to Amazon.com to leave a review – All you need to do is type in our book title, "**The Infinite Money Glitch**" on Amazon and you can easily leave a review there.

P.S. Thank you for taking a minute of your time and helping another person out. This means the world to us and the community.

- Sincerely, your friends Adam and Mike

ADAM DEMCHIK & MIKE MANNINO

Wealth Appreciation

By this point, you realize that holding Multi-family for long periods of time increases the cash flow, which also increases the value of the property.

Let's look at something different instead of just forced appreciation, as we talked about in the Cashflow chapter. Let's discuss the natural appreciation of real estate.

A good question to ask would be,

"How much did it cost to build in 1965?"

Well, let's look at the best resource we have possible... Google. I was curious and asked Google,

"How much did it cost to build an average house in the 1960s?"

This is what came up.

The average cost of a new house in the 1960s was $16,500, which was about three times the household's median income of $5,6 The average cost of a new house in December 2014 was $373,50 which is about seven times the median household's income of $53,657. 15, 2015

Petoskey News-Review
https://www.petoskeynews.com › gaylord › 2015/10/15

My, how things have changed: A look at prices from the 60s

    About featured snippets ·   Feedback

$16,500 was the average cost to build a house in the 1960's.

What?!

Don't you wish you could go back in time and buy 10 of them?

Okay, so let's do some quick estimating here.

So, if the average cost to build a house was $16,500, I would estimate it would cost about half of that for one of our units at 1019 Cypress that we talked about previously. So lets dive into that as an example.

1019 Cypress

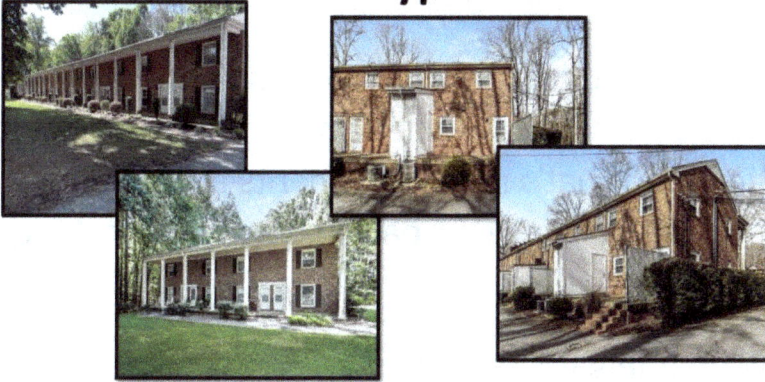

Here's a refresher on what the building looks like. It's a pretty straightforward build, just a long rectangle with a simple roof on a crawl space.

About $8,250 per unit X 16 units = $132,000.

Wow!

Now I really wish I could go back in time and buy 10 of these. Haha. Remember, we just had this property appraised for $1,725,000 by the bank.

So, this property has seen a 13X or 1,300% increase in value from when it was originally built.

Pretty amazing, right?

And, if the original owner had held onto this property, it would have been paid off 30 years ago by the tenants. That's right, our tenants are the ones going to work every day, paying down the mortgage for us.

What if this trend continues?

As we've seen over the last few years with the government printing money, inflation isn't going to stop anytime soon. Just a few years ago, you could have gotten a McDouble for $1.00.

Now, that same product is $2.50.

The dollar menu is pretty much gone at this point.

Let's just say that the current trend continues, and this property grows by 1,300% over the next 60 years.

What will the new value be? Drum roll, please...
🦉 🦉 🦉

$22,425,000!

Mind-blowing, right? 🦁

This is one of the reasons why we typically don't sell our apartment buildings. As you'll read in the **Investment Strategy and Business Plan,** we are long-term investors. We are looking to acquire more of these properties and hold them for a very, very long time.

This is how inflation actually helps the people who own assets that appreciate over time as the value of the dollar decreases.

For fun, let's look at what future rents will be.

$14,300 per month per unit. Wow!

How does real estate create long-term wealth?

Have you ever heard the question:

Would you rather have a penny today, that doubled everyday for a month, or $1 million today? If you haven't heard the answer to this question, you might just jump at the million dollars today without doing the math on taking the penny. Check out the chart below with what happens to your penny doubling everyday.

Day 1	$.01	**Day 16**	$327.68
Day 2	$.02	**Day 17**	$655.36
Day 3	$.04	**Day 18**	$1,310.72
Day 4	$.08	**Day 19**	$2,621.44
Day 5	$.16	**Day 20**	$5,242.88
Day 6	$.32	**Day 21**	$10,485.76
Day 7	$.64	**Day 22**	$20,971.52
Day 8	$1.28	**Day 23**	$41,943.04
Day 9	$2.56	**Day 24**	$83,886.08
Day 10	$5.12	**Day 25**	$167,772.16
Day 11	$10.24	**Day 26**	$335,544.32
Day 12	$20.48	**Day 27**	$671,088.64
Day 13	$40.96	**Day 28**	$1,342,177.28
Day 14	$81.92	**Day 29**	$2,684,354.56
Day 15	$163.84	**Day 30**	$5,368,709.12

I bet you're pretty excited now about that penny! The key here is the concept of compounding interest or compounding returns, which you are probably familiar with. In case you aren't, it's the simple concept that once you gain a return on an investment, you will then gain a return on the original investment, plus a return on the gain.

So in the penny example, the original investment was $.01 and your gain was 100% which got you $.02. The next day you made another 100% return but this time on the $.02 so you ended up with $.04.

How does this apply to real estate? Let's check out the example below of how 1 property could have brought in massive wealth!

Adam's Perspective:

One of the worst things an investor can do is look bad on their previous deals and question their decision. As they say, "hindsight is 20/20". That doesn't mean though that we can learn from a mistake.

"The only real mistake is the one from which we learn nothing."

— Henry Ford

Looking back at one of my previous deals will help show the amazing benefit of how I could have gained several million dollars of multifamily apartments.

Remember that first building I talked about that got me really interested in investing?

To bring you up to speed, I purchased a 48 unit building in Holly, MI in 2013. I used $300,000 of my own money plus a bank loan to purchase the property. I then spent 4 years improving the property.

To increase the NOI (Net Operating Income) of the property, I did the following:

- Renovated 6 vacant units
- Built out the storage and office space into 2 rentable units
- Lightly renovated units when tenants moved out, which increased rents
- Reduced the property taxes by 30%
- Reduced water usage through new fixtures and toilets
- Reduced electricity though motion sensors

To change the culture of the property, I did the following:

- New roof on 1 of the 3 buildings
- Onsite manager
- Updated landscaping
- Fixed the parking lot
- Trimmed trees and brush

After all was done, the property value had just about doubled on paper due to my work and the fact that the market had gone up.

So when I received an unsolicited offer in 2017 for over double what I paid for the property, I took it! In fact, it was about $200,000 more than I thought it was worth at the time.

It was a game changer for my family.

But, did I make the best decision for my family and long term wealth appreciation? **Probably not.**

In hindsight, I had a few options I could have considered with the property. While the option I chose wasn't a bad option, it wasn't the best option.

Below are the options I had when I sold the property. Let's see which one you think is best:

1. Sell the property and take all the profit and original investment and earn 15% every year on it. This would provide me with $200,000 of income every year.
2. Sell the property and purchase another property utilizing a 1031 tax deferred exchange (more about this later, but the premise is you get to pay $0 tax on

the sale of a property as long as you buy another of greater value). The property I would have purchased was a 54 unit property in Lake Orion, MI.

3. Keep the property and refinance it. Use the "Infinite Money Glitch" to keep my cash flowing property with zero of my original capital and purchase another property (I also get to put my original $300,000 investment back in my pocket). The property I would have purchased was a 54 unit property in Lake Orion, MI.

Now which one of these seems like the **BEST** option?

If you guessed #3, you are correct! I missed out on the benefits of the "Infinite Money Glitch" and the chance to build wealth for my family because I picked #1.

Here's a quick snapshot of how #3 would have been the best choice. Try to stay with me because there is a **multi-million dollar lesson** that I learned so you don't have to!

First off, I was cash flowing about $120,000 annually from the Holly property when I sold it. So in my mind option #1 (the $200,000 of interest) sounded great, no tenants and I almost double my annual cash flow.

Choosing #3 would have increased my mortgage payment due to the refinance process and dropped my cash flow to $80,000 but would have allowed me to purchase the 54 unit property described above with the proceeds of the refinance. At the time, it would have brought in about $100,000 in cash flow per year. So the total cash flow would have been $180,000.

So again, #1 still sounds pretty good! But, to illustrate this point, let's jump forward 4 years to 2021 to see where I would be at.

I would now own the 48 unit and the 54 unit. The combined cashflow would be near $220,000. The total value of the two buildings would have gone from about $4,700,000 to about $6,000,000 in value and I would have about $2.5 million of debt on them.

What does that mean? Time for another refinance and another "Infinite Money Glitch".

This is where the numbers get almost unbelievable, so stay with me.

Refinancing the two properties at a 75% LTV (Loan to value) would allow me to get a total loan for $4,500,000. This would give me about $2,000,000 to spend on another building which when using a bank loan at 75% LTV again, I could purchase an $8,000,000 building!

Assuming $60,000 per unit value that $8 million buys me 133 more units for a combined 235 units at a value of $14,000,000 in 2021.

This is all from my original $300,000 investment that I would have put back in my pocket in 2017!

Recap, I own 235 cash flowing units at a total value of $14,000,000 with none of my original investment into them?

That's the **"Infinite Money Glitch"**!

We can't stop the story in 2021! Let's talk about where my portfolio would be in 2024.

Due to Forced Appreciation and Natural Appreciation my $14,000,000 portfolio would now be worth nearly $18,00,000 and the cash flow would be $423,000!!!

With $0 of my own money invested into any of it!

Wait, what? I told you it was almost unbelievable. 😁

Sorry to do it again to you but there's still more!

Not only would I be earning $423,000 per year with #3 and the "Infinite Money Glitch" instead of the $200,000 I was earning with #1, I would be paying almost $0 in taxes on the $423,000 instead of standard tax rates on the $200,000.

But how would I avoid paying taxes on $423,000?

I'm glad you asked. We are going to cover that right now.

Depreciation, 1031, and Tax Benefits

First things first. We purchase, own, and manage apartment buildings. We specialize in that very specific aspect of real estate. We are not tax experts or even real estate tax experts. What we do know is how to use the tax code to our advantage to legally and ethically pay less or no taxes. So, please consult a CPA or tax advisor for your specific situation. What we are providing in this section is our direct experience with the tax advantages of real estate.

Mike's Perspective: Have you ever wondered how the super wealthy don't pay income tax?

We hear about it all the time, but how do they **ACTUALLY** do it?

It's funny, when I first started becoming very successful flipping houses, I quickly found something out: **you always have a money problem.**

When you don't have money, that's an obvious problem because we need basic necessities like food, shelter, clothing, and transportation.

But when you start making a lot of money, you have a new problem: Uncle Sam wants to take half of it.

I was smacked one day with an income tax bill of over $100,000!

Yikes.

At that point, I was determined to find out how the super-wealthy pay less in taxes.

It's kind of funny and sad that my own CPA didn't have an answer for me.

So, I started joining groups, traveling, and networking with super successful people to find out what they do. Here are some of the legal and ethical ways that real estate can help reduce your tax burden.

There are actually many ways to reduce your tax implications, but we are going to cover 3 of the top ones that we use.

(Please read the disclaimer inside of this book that we are not CPAs or tax advisors. This information is just our experience.)

Depreciation:

The IRS requires property owners to depreciate property over 27.5 years. But what does that mean?

Sticking with the 1019 Cypress example.

We paid $900,000 for the property.

We can depreciate the property, excluding the land value, over 27.5 years.

Land Value: $135,000

This leaves $765,000 to be depreciated over 27.5 years.

$765,000 / 27.5 = $27,818

Okay, so what does this mean and why do they do this? <u>Because isn't the property supposed to be making money, not losing money?</u>

Well, the IRS knows that things don't last forever—flooring, cabinets, lights, switches, vanities, toilets, bathtubs, etc.

These things break down and deteriorate over time.

So we get the opportunity to write this off our income every year.

Now that we have 1019 Cypress with increased rents and refinanced, we are making about $41,000 per year.

We can now depreciate about $27,818 of our income.

Now, we are left paying taxes on only $13,000 because we are depreciating on paper everything that deteriorates over time.

So even though we are making $41,000, we are only paying taxes on $13,000.

Does that make sense? I know it's kind of different to grasp the depreciation concept.

Cost Segregation Study:

A cost segregation study is a beautiful thing. As stated above, the IRS requires property owners to depreciate multifamily property over 27.5 years.

A Cost Segregation study or Cost SEG allows the owner of the property to depreciate items in the property MUCH faster than 27.5 years.

Think about it, **how long does carpet last?** With tenants, 3 years max!

There are a ton of other items to include as well.

Back when we purchased the property in 2022, we called up CORE, which is a company that does this for us.

All you really have to know as an investor is that you pay them $5,000.

Then, they come out to the property and work their magic through an engineering study.

They take photos and notes of the entire property and write an extremely detailed 50+ page report.

Okay, brace yourself. It might look kind of shocking at first. Then, as you read through it, it's not too bad. They are just listing everything in great detail and giving everything a Tax Life.

Here's what one of the pages looks like.

Division/Level #	Description	Tax Life	Final Costs	5 Year Property	15 Year Property	27.5 Year Property
04 00 00	Masonry	27.5	$ 118,495.81	$ -	$ -	$ 118,495.81
04 00 00.15	Masonry, Site	15	$ 2,341.34	$ -	$ 2,341.34	$ -
06 00 00	Wood, Plastics, and Composites	27.5	$ 142,394.12	$ -	$ -	$ 142,394.12
06 10 00	Rough Carpentry	27.5	$ 31,723.96	$ -	$ -	$ 31,723.96
06 22 13	Wood Trim	5	$ 454.74	$ 454.74	$ -	$ -
06 25 00	Prefinished Paneling	5	$ 7,510.50	$ 7,510.50	$ -	$ -
07 00 00	Thermal and Moisture Protection	27.5	$ 35,234.62	$ -	$ -	$ 35,234.62
09 50 00	Ceilings	27.5	$ 14,408.74	$ -	$ -	$ 14,408.74
09 60 00	Flooring	27.5	$ 38,799.86	$ -	$ -	$ 38,799.86
09 62 19	Laminate Flooring	5	$ 156.29	$ 156.29	$ -	$ -
09 64 00	Wood Plank Thin Flooring	5	$ 49,564.56	$ 49,564.56	$ -	$ -
09 65 00	VCT	5	$ 296.82	$ 296.82	$ -	$ -
10 14 00.02	Signage, Distributive Trade	5	$ 186.93	$ 186.93	$ -	$ -
10 55 23.15	Mail Boxes	15	$ 1,650.30	$ -	$ 1,650.30	$ -
10 57 23	Closet and Utility Shelving	5	$ 4,046.67	$ 4,046.67	$ -	$ -
12 21 00	Window Blinds	5	$ 1,170.31	$ 1,170.31	$ -	$ -
12 30 00	Casework	5	$ 20,262.53	$ 20,262.53	$ -	$ -
12 36 00	Countertops	5	$ 3,497.37	$ 3,497.37	$ -	$ -
22 00 00	Plumbing	27.5	$ 37,309.94	$ -	$ -	$ 37,309.94
22 10 00.04	Plumbing for Food Service / Kitchen Equipment	5	$ 15,037.41	$ 15,037.41	$ -	$ -
22 10 00.09	Plumbing for Laundry Equipment	5	$ 4,551.92	$ 4,551.92	$ -	$ -
22 10 00.10	Plumbing for Qualified Equipment	5	$ 8,501.39	$ 8,501.39	$ -	$ -
22 10 00.15	Plumbing, Piping and Pumps, Site	15	$ 1,695.81	$ -	$ 1,695.81	$ -
23 00 00	Heating, Ventilating, and Air Conditioning (HVAC)	27.5	$ 47,792.31	$ -	$ -	$ 47,792.31
23 30 00.08	HVAC Air Distribution for Process Equipment	5	$ 1,258.22	$ 1,258.22	$ -	$ -
23 38 00	HVAC Ventilation Hoods	5	$ 792.57	$ 792.57	$ -	$ -
26 00 00	Electrical	27.5	$ 41,987.09	$ -	$ -	$ 41,987.09
26 27 13.05	Meter Center for Qualified Equipment	5	$ 1,219.01	$ 1,219.01	$ -	$ -
26 27 26.01	Wiring Devices for Data / Data Handling Equipment	5	$ 2,062.03	$ 2,062.03	$ -	$ -
26 27 26.02	Wiring Devices for Communication Equipment	5	$ 2,062.03	$ 2,062.03	$ -	$ -
26 27 26.04	Wiring Devices for Food Service/Kitchen Equipment	5	$ 3,753.55	$ 3,753.55	$ -	$ -
26 27 26.06	Wiring Devices for Television Equipment	5	$ 2,062.03	$ 2,062.03	$ -	$ -
26 27 26.09	Wiring Devices for Laundry Equipment	5	$ 1,446.03	$ 1,446.03	$ -	$ -
26 27 26.10	Wiring Devices for Qualifying Equipment	5	$ 6,739.74	$ 6,739.74	$ -	$ -
26 27 26.15	Wiring Devices for Site Equipment	15	$ 691.29	$ -	$ 691.29	$ -
26 27 73	Door Chimes	5	$ 2,209.85	$ 2,209.85	$ -	$ -
26 28 16.01	Switches and Breakers for Data / Data Handling Equipment	5	$ 364.48	$ 364.48	$ -	$ -
26 28 16.02	Switches and Breakers for Communications Equipment	5	$ 364.48	$ 364.48	$ -	$ -
26 28 16.04	Switches and Breakers for Food/Kitchen Equipment	5	$ 850.46	$ 850.46	$ -	$ -
26 28 16.06	Switches and Breakers for Television Equipment	5	$ 364.48	$ 364.48	$ -	$ -
26 28 16.09	Switches and Breakers for Laundry Equipment	5	$ 1,021.06	$ 1,021.06	$ -	$ -
26 28 16.10	Switches and Breakers for Qualifying Equipment	5	$ 1,866.71	$ 1,866.71	$ -	$ -
26 28 16.15	Switches and Breakers for Site Equipment	15	$ 102.56	$ -	$ 102.56	$ -
26 56 29	Site Lighting	15	$ 1,067.84	$ -	$ 1,067.84	$ -
27 20 00	Outlet, Data / Data Handling	5	$ 2,239.24	$ 2,239.24	$ -	$ -
27 30 00	Voice Communications Outlets	5	$ 1,610.96	$ 1,610.96	$ -	$ -
27 40 00	Audio-Video Communications	5	$ 2,287.57	$ 2,287.57	$ -	$ -
31 23 16	Excavation	27.5	$ 10,826.50	$ -	$ -	$ 10,826.50
31 60 00	Foundation	27.5	$ 18,366.44	$ -	$ -	$ 18,366.44
32 12 16	Asphalt Paving	15	$ 31,153.03	$ -	$ 31,153.03	$ -
32 13 13	Concrete Paving	15	$ 15,517.86	$ -	$ 15,517.86	$ -
32 30 00	Site Improvements	15	$ 384.96	$ -	$ 384.96	$ -
32 31 00	Fences and Gates	15	$ 3,403.78	$ -	$ 3,403.78	$ -
32 93 00	Landscaping	15	$ 19,839.89	$ -	$ 19,839.89	$ -
	Total - Building Costs		$ 765,000.00	$ 149,811.94	$ 77,848.67	$ 537,339.39
	Allocated Percentage		100.00%	19.58%	10.18%	70.24%
	Land/Non-Depreciable		$ 135,000.00			
	Grand Total - Cost Segregation Analysis		$ 900,000.00			

If you look at a lot of the items, they are only given a 5-year tax life. Wood trim, flooring, window blinds, countertops, and some plumbing and electrical items.

They have everything totaling up to $765,000, leaving out the land value of $135,000, which brings us to our total purchase price of $900,000.

What does all of this mean?

Well, with the Cost Seg report detailing everything, we were able to deduct **$227,661 from our taxes in year 1.**

You read that right. We were able to claim a depreciation amount of **$227,661!**

The first year we owned this property, we were able to make a $227,661 deduction from our taxes.

<u>See the benefit of paying that company $5,000?</u>

Now, with our $41,000 in profit, we have $227,661 = -$186,661 left over to deduct from our taxes.

With us considered real estate professionals, we are able to even carry that extra $186,661 to our other income.

Let's say Mike made $186,661 flipping houses in a year.

He's able to deduct that from his income and show $0 for the year.

Mind blown again? 🐯

This right here is one of the biggest secrets of how the wealthy don't pay income taxes.

1031 Exchange

1031 Exchanges might sound like some *obscure tax code idea*. Once you throw the numbers into the name, everything sounds **way** more complicated.

Actually, they are very simple and the biggest way real estate investors transfer wealth to successive generations.

In the simplest explanation, they defer capital gains taxes to a later time. So, if you sell a property for a profit, you can defer or postpone being taxed on that gain as long as you purchase another property that meets the following conditions:

1. It's more expensive.

2. It's an investment property.

3. You complete a timeline of events and complete the purchase within 6 months.

So, you can legally get taxed on any gain you make selling a property later down the line. While this doesn't sound like a big deal, imagine buying and selling multiple properties for a profit several times over a 30 or 40-year period. Those gains would compound as you would be using the deferred tax monies to purchase bigger and bigger properties.

So when do you eventually pay the tax, since this is a deferred tax, remember? Well, if you plan it correctly, **NEVER**.

You die with a huge **deferred tax amount**!

"Our new Constitution is now established and has an appearance that promises permanency, but in this world, nothing can be said to be certain, except death and taxes."

—Benjamin Franklin, in a letter to <u>Jean-Baptiste Le Roy</u>, 1789

Ben Franklin was only right about one of those. We are all definitely going to die, but if we die with a huge tax bill, you never have to pay it!

Here's the kicker...whomever you leave the property to gets to wipe out the entire deferred tax amount, and the cost basis of the property is reset to the current value!

Adam's Perspective:

The power of deferring large amounts of taxable income through a 1031 exchange can seem like a daunting task, given you are dealing with tax codes. But in truth, it's pretty simple. There are some fantastic companies that help through the whole process and have streamlined the paperwork.

In 2021, I sold my favorite building, a 4-unit property in a growing town. I never intended on selling it as it was across from Dairy Queen and on the parade route for the Peach Festival. But, when I had the opportunity to defer taxes on a $150,000 gain, I jumped at the opportunity.

Through cold calling, I found a 10-unit building down the street from my 4-unit. It was well cared for and had great tenants already in place. It had a few advantages over my 4-unit that I found very attractive:

1. It was not in the village of Romeo, so the taxes per unit were lower.

2. It was a purpose-built apartment complex.

3. It had onsite laundry, which is a bonus for tenant retention.

Once under contract, I quickly listed my 4-unit for sale and received several offers. I took the offer with the highest down payment and called my 1031 exchange company. They facilitated all the necessary paperwork to transfer the proceeds of my 4-unit sale to their escrow account, and then when I was ready to purchase my 10-unit, they transferred the funds in for closing.

Here are the numbers of how this all worked:

- Purchased the 4-unit for $120,000 in 2014 with $40,000 down and a personal loan from family for the remaining $80,000.

- Refinanced the 4-unit in 2020, getting a loan for $131,000. I paid back my family member's loan and put the remaining $51,000 back into my bank account…kinda like an infinite money glitch before I knew that I was doing it!

- Sold my 4-unit in 2021, paid off the $131,000 loan, and transferred $122,000 to my 1031 exchange company which held the funds until my 10-unit purchase was ready.

- Completed the purchase of my 10-unit property using the $122,000 held by my 1031 exchange company and bringing $54,000 in cash to close.

That's right…remember above I put the $51,000 back in the bank a year earlier after my refinance? That means I purchased my 10-unit property with a total down payment of $54,000 out of pocket!

Investment Strategy and Business Plan

"The future belongs to those who believe in the beauty of their dreams."

– Eleanor Roosevelt.

We have discussed the reasons why multifamily real estate, cash flow, wealth appreciation, and the tax benefits of real estate are so compelling. When you combine all of these factors, it becomes clear that multifamily real estate is a very powerful vehicle.

Mike's Perspective: After flipping over 90 houses by now, I realized there was a ton of money left on the table. I remember my first house, which I bought at 19 years old from a foreclosure back in 2012, for only $67,000.

I fixed it up and lived in the house for 2.5 years. Then, at 22 years old, I sold that same house for $147,000, making a substantial profit that really helped kick off my flipping career. But looking back...

My mortgage for that house was $595 per month, and now that same house is worth north of $250,000, leaving a total of $100,000 in equity behind. It could easily be rented out for $1,800/month.

It's funny; every successful real estate investor I've met has said the same thing:

"My biggest regret was selling my rentals."

Now, I wouldn't go as far as saying that I regret selling all of my properties. But there are definitely several I should have held onto.

Adam's and my investment strategy is to buy properties in stable and growing areas, purchase them below market value, force the appreciation as quickly as possible, then refinance the property to get all of our investors' initial capital back out and hold onto them for a very long time for the cash flow, tax benefits, and wealth appreciation using the Infinite Money Glitch over and over.

If you would like to see some of our other properties, check out our website.

Checkout The List of Our Multi-family Properties:
https://www.reciprocitycg.com/our-properties

BRRRR

When you hear BRRR, you probably think of a winter storm. But this is actually an acronym for a type of real estate investing strategy.

Buy, Rehabilitate, Rent, Refinance and Repeat. (BRRR)

This is a real estate investor terminology for buying properties, fixing them up, going back to the bank to get your initial capital back, and repeating the process.

Just like we did for the 1019 Cypress property.

Where we bought the property, fixed it up, forced the appreciation, and went back to the bank to get our initial capital back.

What I didn't tell you was that $420,000 we got back from the bank.

We actually invested a portion of that money directly into a 44-unit apartment in Paducah, Kentucky, that we bought with our investors.

Interested in the idea of Investing with us? Click here if you are on the digital version or enter the website link below to fill out a short questionnaire and book a 1-on-1 call with Mike and Adam. https://www.reciprocitycg.com/start-investing

Now, we've scaled the money invested from a 16-unit property to a total of 60 units.

Guess what we're going to do in two more years after we're done forcing the appreciation of the new 44-unit property in Kentucky?

Go back to the bank, get our initial investment back, and buy another property. We'll keep stacking the monthly cash flow, depreciation, and wealth appreciation over and over again.

Adam learned his lesson on selling his 48 unit property and won't make that mistake again!

Business Plan

We have a simple business plan of buying multi-family properties in steady and growing economies. We are looking for businesses moving to the area, which will bring jobs and people.

We also look for local governments that are landlord-friendly, low crime, and safe places with good schools. We default to if we had to live on the property, would we feel safe?

Not every economy is created equal.

Even though Adam and Mike are from Michigan, and started investing there, we are looking for properties in other states that are growing.

Since COVID happened, many people began working from home and have been packing up and moving south where it's warmer. That's exactly what Mike did in 2022.

The U.S. States Losing & Gaining Population

Population growth by U.S. state from 2022 to 2023*

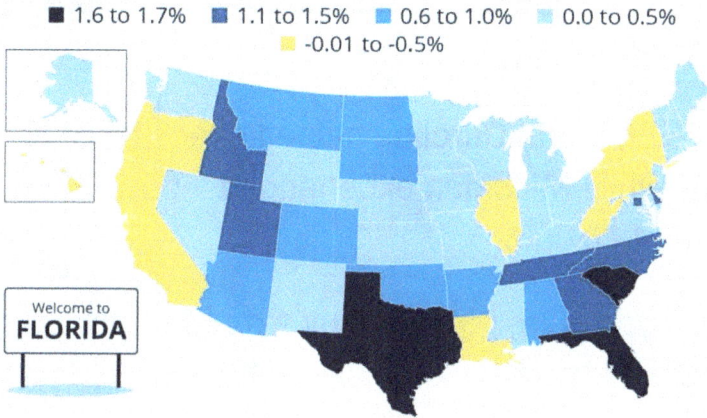

- 1.6 to 1.7%
- 1.1 to 1.5%
- 0.6 to 1.0%
- 0.0 to 0.5%
- -0.01 to -0.5%

Welcome to
FLORIDA

* As of mid-year
Source: U.S. Census Bureau

statista

Source: https://www.statista.com/chart/12484/population-growth-in-the-united-states-by-federal-state/

Here's the map of the United States showing the population growth by state from 2022 to 2023.

Notice that the east and west coasts are losing population, and the Midwest is experiencing relatively flat growth.

Look at states like Tennessee, North Carolina, South Carolina, and Georgia. Those are dark blue or black, indicating over a 1.1% to 1.7% positive change in population in just one year.

This trend has been ongoing for a while, but since 2020, it has really picked up.

In 2022, North Carolina gained over +100,000 people, while Michigan experienced a population decline of 10,000.

So, if you were going to buy a multi-family property and hold it for a very long time, where should you invest?

In the Midwest, where there's stagnant growth? Or in the south, where people and businesses are moving to?

The answer is pretty simple and clear. We want the demand of people moving to where our properties are located so that the natural appreciation of the property's value happens quickly.

One of the reasons Mike moved to South Carolina is so that he can be on the ground, acquiring, managing renovations, and checking on the property's performance.

We will discuss more about the details of how we choose the right property, which we call **"The Horse."**

For now, I think you get a good understanding of the significance of the property's location and being on the growth side and how that helps future appreciation and cash flow.

You can grab yourself a copy of the Sample Deal Package here:
https://www.reciprocitycg.com/sample-deal-package

Different Asset Classes

In real estate, there are asset classes for both the property and the neighborhood. Starting with

(A), which represents the best. These neighborhoods would have the best schools, lowest crime rates, and high demand for the land. You will typically see in these neighborhoods where developers are removing older homes and building multi-million dollar properties. These areas are great for appreciation but are generally terrible for cash flow because the property values are so high.

(D) Being the worst, these would be your Detroit or Flint, Michigan where schools aren't great, there is high crime, high poverty, and low demand for the land. You will typically see infill lots sitting vacant because no one wants to build in these neighborhoods. We avoid these neighborhoods like the plague.

We invest in B and C neighborhoods with stability, good schools, low poverty, and demand for real estate intersect. A crucial question to ask is how we would feel living or walking around there at night. If the answer is anything less than feeling safe, it doesn't matter how promising the numbers look on paper for the property. We skip and move on to the next one, because attracting quality tenants who want to live there will be challenging.

Now, let's delve deeper into the definitions of the A, B, C, and D classes for both the property and the neighborhood:

1. **Class A Multi-family:**

- *Property:* Typically newer or recently renovated buildings with high-end amenities and finishes. They boast modern designs, upscale appliances, and high-quality materials. Situated in desirable neighborhoods, they command higher rents.

- *Neighborhood:* Characterized by low crime rates, good school districts, and proximity to amenities such as employment centers, shopping, and entertainment. They offer a high quality of life and are often in urban or suburban areas with strong economic fundamentals.

2. **Class B Multi-family:**

- *Property:* Generally well-maintained, older buildings that may have been renovated to some extent. They offer decent amenities and comfortable living spaces, albeit lacking some luxury features. Rents are typically lower than Class A but higher than Class C and D.

- *Neighborhood:* Stable with moderate crime rates and good access to amenities. They may not be as upscale or desirable as Class A neighborhoods but they attract a mix of middle-income families, young professionals, and retirees.

3. **Class C Multi-family:**

- *Property:* Older buildings require more maintenance and upkeep, often lacking modern amenities. Rents are lower compared to Class A and B, making them more affordable for lower-income tenants.

- *Neighborhood:* This neighborhood may have higher crime rates and fewer amenities than Class A and B neighborhoods. Often located in transitional areas undergoing redevelopment or gentrification. They offer more affordable housing options but may have higher vacancy rates and turnover.

4. **Class D Multi-family:**

- *Property:* Typically older, poorly maintained buildings in need of significant renovation or repair. Lacking basic amenities, they may have safety, sanitation, or structural issues. Rents are the lowest among all classes.

- *Neighborhood:* Characterized by high crime rates, limited access to amenities, and economic distress. Often have vacant or abandoned properties, and residents face socio-economic challenges such as poverty and unemployment. Investing in Class D properties and neighborhoods involves higher risk and may require substantial investment to improve.

Property Sizes and Mix

Now, let's discuss the size of properties we typically seek. In the realm of Multi-family, a property can range from as small as a duplex, which consists of two units, to large complexes with over 1,000 units. However, each size category comes with its own set of pros and cons.

Mike's Perspective:

Our company, Reciprocity Capital Group, typically targets properties in the 20 - 100 unit range. This range aligns with our goals to accelerate appreciation as swiftly as possible, and thus, we target a specific type of property aligned with our Investment Strategy and Business plan.

Let's continue:

1. **2 - 4 Units:**

- *Pros:* • Typically easier to finance, especially for individual investors. • More affordable for those starting in real estate. • Allows owner-occupants to live in one unit while renting out others.

- *Cons:* • Limited scalability, requiring more management overhead. • Less economies of scale, leading to higher operating expenses per unit. • Limited rental income potential compared to larger properties.

2. **5 - 20 Units:**

- *Pros:* • Manageable for individual investors or small investment groups. • Offers some economies of scale compared to smaller properties. • Provides a balance between cash flow and scalability.

- *Cons:* • Increased management intensity due to more tenants and potential maintenance issues. • Limited financing options, potentially higher interest rates. • Less diversification compared to larger properties.

3. **21 - 100 Units:**

- *Pros:* • Greater economies of scale, resulting in lower operating costs per unit. • Still manageable for smaller investors, offering the potential for cash flow and appreciation. • Balance between scalability and operational complexity.

- *Cons:* • Requires more sophisticated management and investment strategies. • Financing may be more complex, though numerous options exist. • Higher market competition compared to smaller properties.

4. **100+ Units:**

- *Pros:* • Significant economies of scale, lower operating costs, and greater cash flow potential. • Typically professionally managed, offering the potential for appreciation and diversification. • Higher potential for appreciation and portfolio growth.

- *Cons:* • High barriers to entry due to substantial upfront capital requirements. • More complex financing and stricter loan requirements. • Greater market sensitivity to economic downturns or market fluctuations.

By targeting properties in the 20 - 100 unit range, we aim to leverage economies of scale while maintaining manageable complexity and maximizing appreciation potential. This strategy allows us to optimize cash flow, minimize risk, and achieve long-term investment success.

Active investing vs. Passive investing

Active Investing

Mike's Perspective:

Education: If you want to become an active investor, you will first want to start off with your education. Congratulations! You are doing that right now 👏

Although this is a great stepping stone in your education, this is just the beginning. You will have to join and be surrounded by high-level individuals so that you are up to date on what's going on in the marketplace.

Here's a photo I took last year. This is a photo of some of the lanyards I have received from live events I've traveled the world to accumulate. At this point of writing this book, I've spent over $150,000 on self-education in real estate and marketing. This also excludes the $65,000 I spent on college.

I make it a point to always be on top of the cutting edge and what's going on in the marketplace for my investors. As they trust me to operate the deals with their retirement money, I take that role very seriously.

Adam's Perspective:

Investing in any business or asset comes with a learning curve. In my view, multi-family real estate falls on the easier end of the spectrum, but having a mentor or teacher who has navigated through various challenges and understands best practices is invaluable.

Investing also demands time. Regardless of what you've observed, some level of effort and time investment is necessary. Collaborating with *seasoned professional investors* can significantly streamline the process. We've all heard the horror stories of troublesome tenants damaging units or dealing with midnight water leaks. While these incidents do occur, with experience, such challenges become opportunities to resolve issues and enhance the property.

If you would like to work with Mike 1-on-1 being an active investor, click this link if you are on the digital version of the book or type in this URL to book a call: https://www.rewbuilders.com/book-a-call

Mike's Perspective:

Deal Sourcing:

Deal sourcing is one of the most critical aspects of being an active investor, yet it's not an easy task. Many newcomers mistakenly believe they can find profitable deals simply by browsing platforms like Zillow or LoopNet. Unfortunately, the reality is different.

In this <u>fiercely competitive</u> market, online listings are often already picked over by more sophisticated investors, leaving the leftovers for newbies to get burned on.

In our business, we allocate over **$100,000 annually** from our own funds to advertising in order to find discounted real estate. <u>Yes, you read that right</u>—we spend six figures per year on sourcing discounted real estate. We utilize various channels such as direct print media, social media, wholesalers, brokers, investment groups, niche listing sites, and Google PPC. Within our company, Bryce and Glen are dedicated to scouring the internet, engaging with brokers/wholesalers, and evaluating potential deals.

Taking a glance at our Key Performance Indicators (KPIs), we review approximately 350 deals per month but only proceed to purchase 1-2 deals per year.

This means we evaluate a staggering **4,000 deals annually** but only execute a small fraction of them. Being a deal finder requires significant activity and is like having a full-time job, demanding a considerable portion of our financial resources and energy.

Now, let's dive into other crucial aspects of active investing:

Financial Analysis:

Understanding financial calculators and metrics such as Cap Rates, Cash on Cash Returns, Internal Rate of Returns, conducting thorough financial analyses of potential deals, and assessing risk factors are pivotal. More insights on what we scrutinize in the "**Horse Vs The Jockey**" chapter.

Negotiation:

Negotiating purchase terms with sellers involves discussing price, financial contingencies, physical contingencies, taxes, closing costs, timelines, and due diligence periods. It's crucial to ensure contracts are written correctly to avoid exploitation by sophisticated investors and attorneys. Engaging an attorney to draft and review contracts is highly advisable.

Due Diligence:

During the due diligence period, comprehensive scrutiny of the property and its financials is essential. This includes physical inspections, structural, plumbing, and wiring assessments, environmental evaluations, financial audits, lease agreements, bank account audits, and market analyses. This phase aims to verify the property's condition, **assess potential risks, and evaluate current and future income and expenses.**

Financing:

When it comes to Multifamily financing and working with banks and investors, there are a few things you need to understand. First is that the lenders will be underwriting the property's ability to pay back the debt on the property. Banks may require financial reports for the property going back 3 years.

Experience is going to be required from either you or someone you are partnering with. Banks will typically require that at least one of the partners buying the property has experience and can show that they have a successful track record of buying and managing multifamily properties.

Not all debt is created equal: Just because a bank says they are willing to finance your purchase doesn't mean you should go with them. There is a lot to understand especially with Multifamily financing options. Prepayment penalties, interest rate adjustments, balloon payments, fixed vs floating interest rates, escrow reserves, and personal guarantees.

Make sure you are working with a mortgage broker who can shop multiple banks for you and explain the differences between each loan. Or you can call multiple banks yourself.

Asset Management:

This is different from property management. In our business, we hire property managers who manage the day-to-day operations dealing with maintenance requests, collecting rents, listing properties for rent and signing new leases.

But just because you hire a property manager doesn't mean your work is done. Now you have to manage them and set clear expectations and KPIs (Key Performance Indicators).

In our company, we meet with each property manager weekly for a live Zoom call and are in constant communication on maintenance requests lease experiences, lease renewals, insurance, unit turns, and rent collections.

Asset Management also requires a lot of travel to the properties multiple times per year. It's good to have one of the owners checking in on the property and making sure the physical condition is safe and clean.

Sourcing and working with contractors: Managing major renovations is also on the Asset Management team. For example, we bought a 19-unit apartment in North Carolina last year. We are doing a major renovation to the property with new kitchens, floors, doors, bathrooms, vanities, windows roofs, and landscaping. This is going to be close to a $300,000 renovation when we are done.

A project like this is a big undertaking. For the interior renovations, I had to call and interview over 35 contractors for the job, making sure we got someone who's licensed, insured, competent, and can work on my time schedule and budget.

Risk Management:

When you are investing millions of dollars in multifamily it's required you have good risk management skills. I see a lot of new investors who get very excited about their first deal and overlook the risks they are taking. Right now a lot of investors are getting burned who bought their properties in 2021 on variable rate mortgages. When they bought, the interest rate was 3%, and the deal worked. But now, rates are close to 7%, and that same dream deal has turned into a nightmare.

Passive Investing

Education:

If you want to be a passive investor, you should still have a good understanding of what you will be investing in. That's why Adam and Mike have written this book—for **YOU**, our current and future investors. We want you to be as educated as possible so that you're confident and knowledgeable in your investments.

Congratulations on investing in your future and in yourself! 🎉

Investment Structure:

Understand the investment structure, such as direct ownership, a Joint Venture, Syndication, or a real estate investment trust.

Risk Profile:

Evaluate the risk profile of the investment, including the property itself, market risk, economic factors, and vacancies in the property. Consider the property's location, condition, tenant demographics, and even understanding the loan attached to the property.

Financial Performance:

Understand the historical financial performance, including cash flow, occupancy, expenses, and projected returns.

Investment Sponsor and Team AKA The Jockey:

This is a big one—make sure to evaluate the track record, experience, and reputation of the investment team. Do they have the experience for their business plan? For example, if the team is planning a major renovation to a property, have they ever done one before?

Make sure that the team's business plan for the property and your own financial plan are aligned. For example, many sponsors and teams like to buy properties, fix them up, and sell them for a profit, continuing to flip properties. However, this takes away from the magic of long-term cash flow and wealth appreciation.

Interested in the idea of Investing with us? Click here if you are on the digital version or enter the website link below to fill out a short questionnaire and book a 1-on-1 call with Mike and Adam. https://www.reciprocitycg.com/start-investing

We will talk more about finding and interviewing the Jockey in the **Horse and Jockey** chapter.

How to Invest

Retirement Accounts:

We wanted to include this chapter because we feel it's very important. Many people believe they can only invest their cash into real estate, but that's far from the truth.

If you have an existing IRA, Roth IRA, 401(K), 403(B), 457 Plan, Thrift Savings Plan (TSP), SEP IRA, SIMPLE IRA, and even some Pension Plans, you can roll over these accounts into what's called a self-directed IRA.

A self-directed IRA (Individual Retirement Account) is a type of retirement account that allows account holders to have greater control over their investment choices compared to traditional IRAs. With a self-directed IRA, individuals can invest in a wide range of alternative assets beyond the typical options offered by traditional IRAs, such as stocks, bonds, and mutual funds. These alternative investments can include real estate, precious metals, private equity, private lending, and more.

Most of the money our investors use to invest in our real estate deals actually comes from their retirement accounts. For example, in our newest purchase in Kentucky, we had our investors use an existing or old 401(K) to invest. However, there is a process you need to follow to make sure you are doing the rollover correctly.

In addition, there are a few rules that must be followed to allow these types of investments to take place. We recommend that you contact one of several self-directed IRA companies to make sure that investing this way is right for you. We use companies like Equity Trust, who will help you with the entire paperwork process, making it seamless.

They have over $45 billion in assets and 334,000+ accounts under custody and administration with 50 years in financial services. We have had dozens of our investors use this company, and they are great to work with.

There are also many other wonderful companies out there that can help with Self Directed IRAs.

Syndications:

Syndication is simply a real estate investment where multiple investors pool their money together collectively to invest in a multi-family property. In syndication, there are typically two main parts involved: the Syndicator (or sponsors/Team AKA Jockey) and the passive Investors.

Syndicator (Sponsor):

The syndicator is the team responsible for sourcing, acquiring, managing, and ultimately realizing the investment potential of the multi-family property. That would be Adam, Mike, and their company at Reciprocity Capital Group. They are the syndicators who are running the operations of the deal.

Passive Investors:

Passive investors are individuals who contribute capital to the syndication but do not actively participate in the day-to-day operations of the property. Passive investors rely on the expertise and efforts of the syndicator to generate returns on their investment. In exchange for their investment, passive investors typically receive ownership interests (equity) in the property and may also receive periodic distributions of income generated by the property.

Syndication is one of the most popular ways for passive investors who want to work with us to participate in the deals we buy and take ownership of.

Our investors get to leverage our experience, time, team, and resources. As we talked about in the **Active Investing section**, you can see there is a lot of work that goes into finding a deal that makes sense and operating it successfully.

We get to help and leverage our investors by putting their capital to work in deals that we couldn't buy ourselves. It's a perfect mutually beneficial relationship working with our investors.

> **Want to learn more about using your retirement accounts to invest in real estate?** Click here if you are on the digital version or enter the website link below to fill out a short questionnaire and book a 1-on-1 call with Mike and Adam.
> https://www.reciprocitycg.com/start-investing

"The way to get started is to quit talking and begin doing."

– Walt Disney.

The Horse vs. the Jockey

We made it to the Horse vs The Jockey. We have talked about it throughout this book for a while. We coined this phrase a few years ago doing a presentation talking to a group of investors about investing in Adam's debt fund, which loans fix and flippers and other multi-family operators money for a short period of time.

This phrase, the Horse Vs. The Jockey seemed like the simplest way to differentiate an investment.

Horse – The Property

What's important about the property? It's crucial to consider factors such as the area, location, population demographics, age, physical condition, income levels, nearby businesses, employment opportunities, crime rates, and quality of schools.

When we are looking at properties to invest in, the first thing we look at is population. Is there a large enough population, and is there a demand for our property?

When looking at the population, you want to look at the trend. Is the population increasing, steady, or decreasing?

Population:

Here's a screenshot of the Kentucky deal we bought in McCracken County. This is from our deal pitch deck that we give to all of our investors.

MARKET FUNDAMENTALS

How many people live in McCracken County?

Population in McCracken County

McCracken County's population **grew 3%** from the **65,523** people who lived there in **2010**. For comparison, the population in the US **grew 7.7%** and the population in Kentucky **grew 3.8%** during that period.

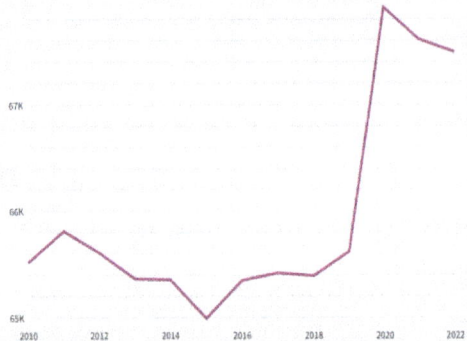

67K

66K

65K

2010   2012   2014   2016   2018   2020   2022

The population of McCracken County, Kentucky in 2022 was 67,490, 3% up from the 65,523 who lived there in 2010. For comparison, the US population grew 7.7% and Kentucky's population grew 3.8% during that period.

This is a healthy graph we want to see, where the population is steady and has been increasing over recent years.

Here is another example of population, but one we do **NOT** want to see. Which is Detroit, Michigan.

620,376 (2022)

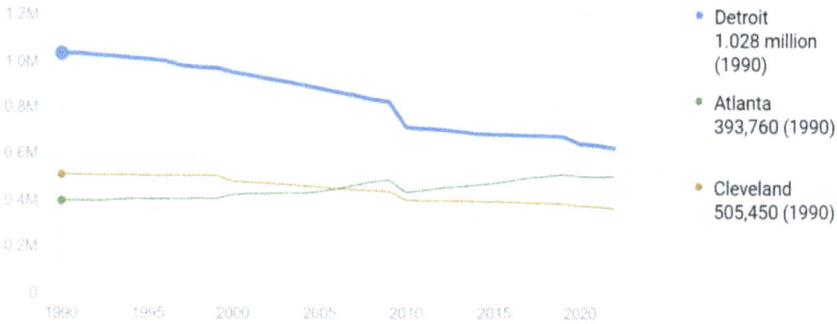

• Detroit	1.028 million (1990)
• Atlanta	393,760 (1990)
• Cleveland	505,450 (1990)

This image was found by Google using the search term 'Detroit Michigan Population.' Notice how in 1990, the city had over 1,000,000 residents, and now there are only 620,000 people. Since COVID, this number has likely dropped even further, possibly to under 600,000 people.

Real estate operates on a simple supply and demand principle. When there are fewer people (demand) for available properties (supply), both property prices and rents tend to decrease.

Employment:

The diversity of employers and job opportunities is crucial because you want to ensure that the area where you're investing has a robust and varied economy.

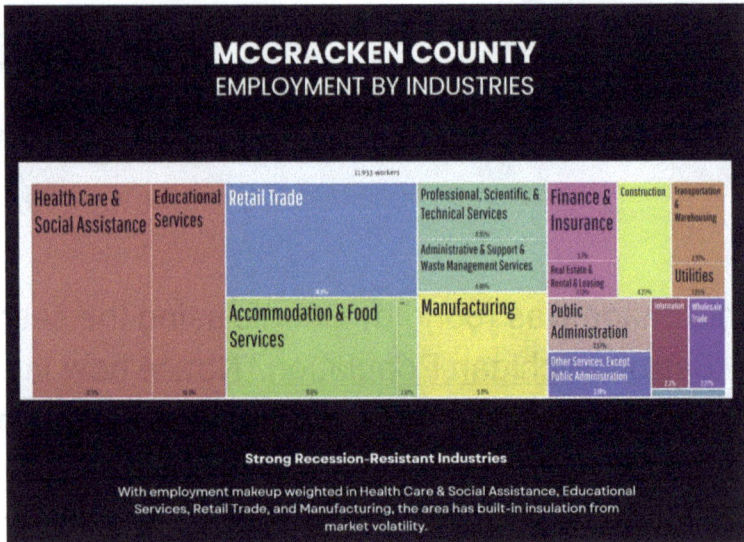

In the Kentucky property we acquired, there is a diverse mix of industries, including healthcare and social assistance, educational services, retail trade, accommodation and food services, manufacturing, and professional, scientific, and technical services.

We aim to avoid areas reliant on a single major employer or dominated by one industry. These are often referred to as 'one-horse towns,' where the entire economy depends on the performance of a single entity.

We have a friend who owned an apartment building in a small town where the primary employer was a beer manufacturing company. Unfortunately, when the company closed its location, it devastated the entire town.

Type of Businesses:

It may sound amusing, but we frequently look for Chick-fil-A and Starbucks locations near our properties. Both companies invest heavily in market research and strategically choose their store locations based on specific criteria, including income levels and population demographics of the area.

Consider this: have you ever seen a Starbucks or Chick-fil-A in a financially struggling neighborhood? The answer is usually no because customers typically require disposable income to afford their products.

Chick-fil-A and Starbucks are both in Paducah. They both have very specific city criteria. Know where people are moving to and income requirements.

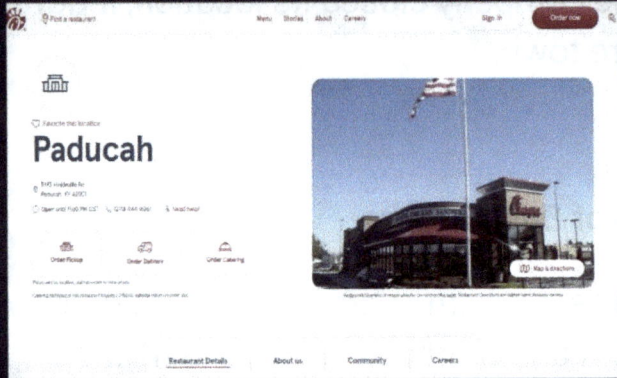

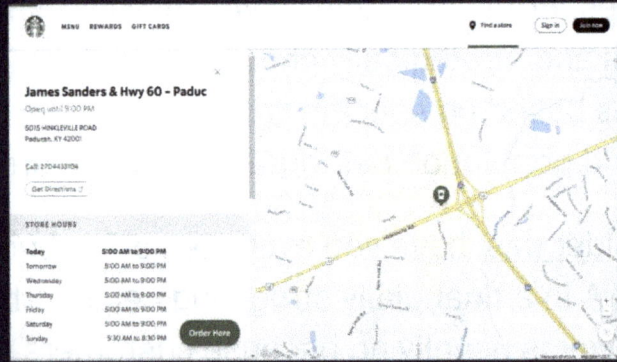

Schools:

Schools are extremely important to the value of the town. If you notice wherever the best schools are, they attract the highest values in price and rent.

In areas that don't have adequate schools, their property values and rents are a lot lower.

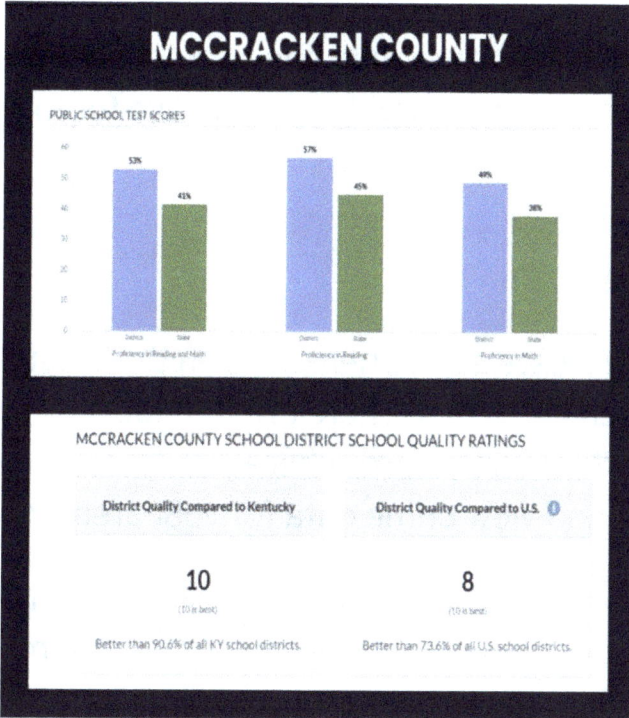

As you can see here, we are measuring the performance of McCracken schools against the state and the country.

In the bar graph, the district performs better in Math and Reading than the rest of the state.

District quality compared to Kentucky: McCracken is better than 90.6% of all other schools in the state.

District quality compared to the U.S. is better than 73.6% of all U.S. schools.

With having better than average schools you can see that this is a desirable place to live for families.

Crime:

Crime exists everywhere, even in the most affluent and expensive areas. There are free tools available, such as SpotCrime.com, where you can enter your address and view crime data for your area.

For example, when examining McCracken County in Kentucky, minimal crime is reported. It's important to delve into the specifics of the crime data to understand the type of the incidents.

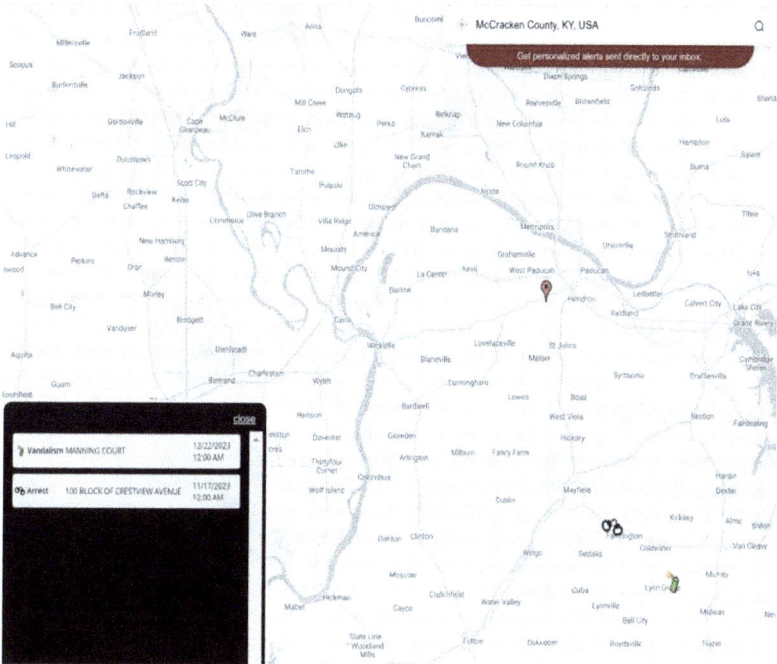

Here there are only two instances that show up - some vandalism and an arrest.

Then you can look at other locations like Memphis, Tennessee.

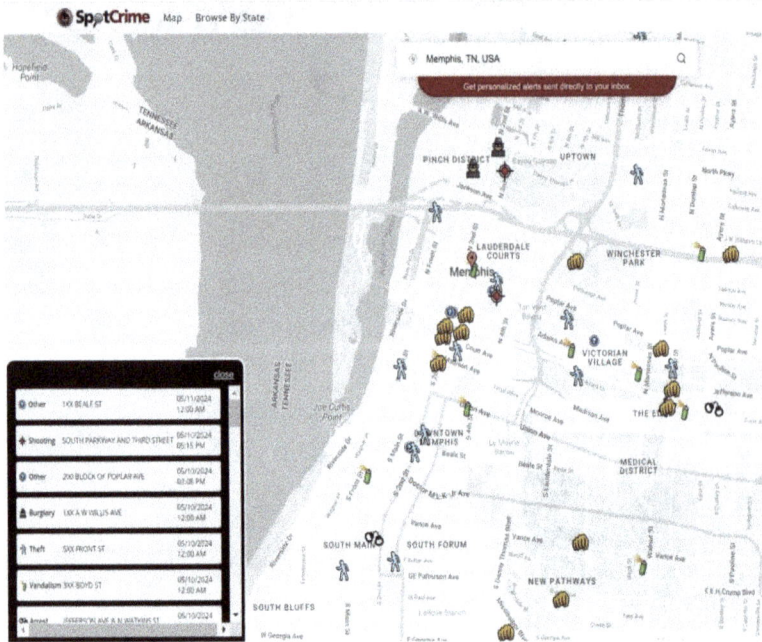

There is an endless list of assaults (that's the first), burglary, and even a few gunshots. These crimes are a lot more common here and more violent than vandalism and an arrest.

Growth and Competition:

What does the new construction industry look like in the market you are looking at?

Is it non-existent, with many older homes built in the 1950s and limited growth? This is common for places with stagnant or a population in decline.

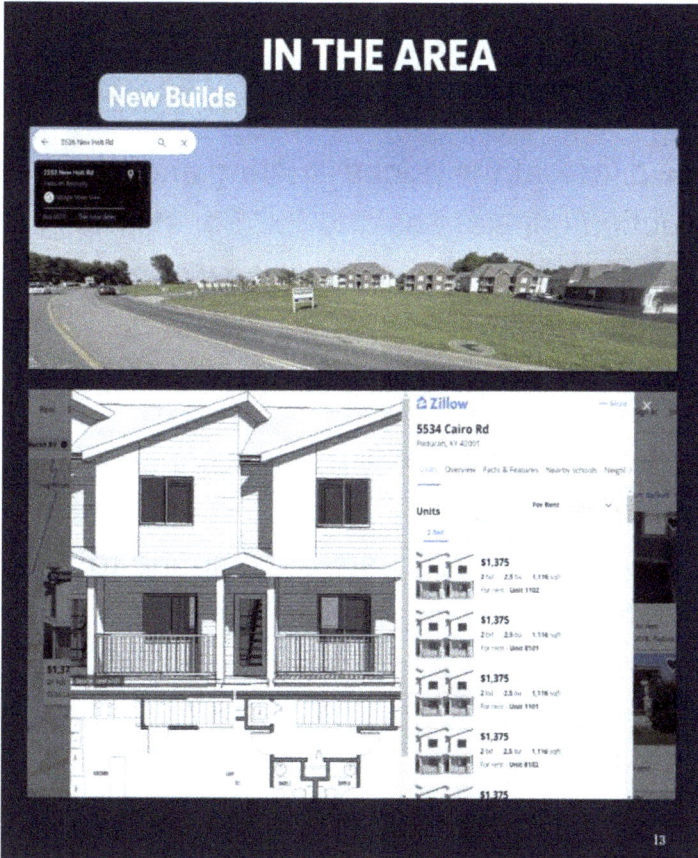

Again, looking at McCracken County, there are new construction houses and apartments in the area confirming that there is growth in this area;

otherwise, builders wouldn't be constructing new properties.

Competition:

Take a look at the prices existing and new construction units are asking for. For example, at the 553 Cairo Rd property, there are new construction apartments renting for $1,375 a month for 2 bed 2.5 bath units that are 1,116 square feet in size.

This indicates a healthy market, especially considering that the 2-bedroom, 1-bath units in the property we purchased were only renting for $580 a month. This suggests there is significant potential to increase our rental rates without reaching the top of the market.

Physical Condition:

Now, what is the physical condition of the property? When was it built, and are there any physical issues or deferred maintenance?

EXTERIOR PICTURES

Continuing with our Kentucky property, which was built in the 1970s with a brick exterior. The exterior of the units were in great condition. We plan on fixing some deferred maintenance like tree trimming, replacing a few roofs, and re-seal coating the parking lot with new lines.

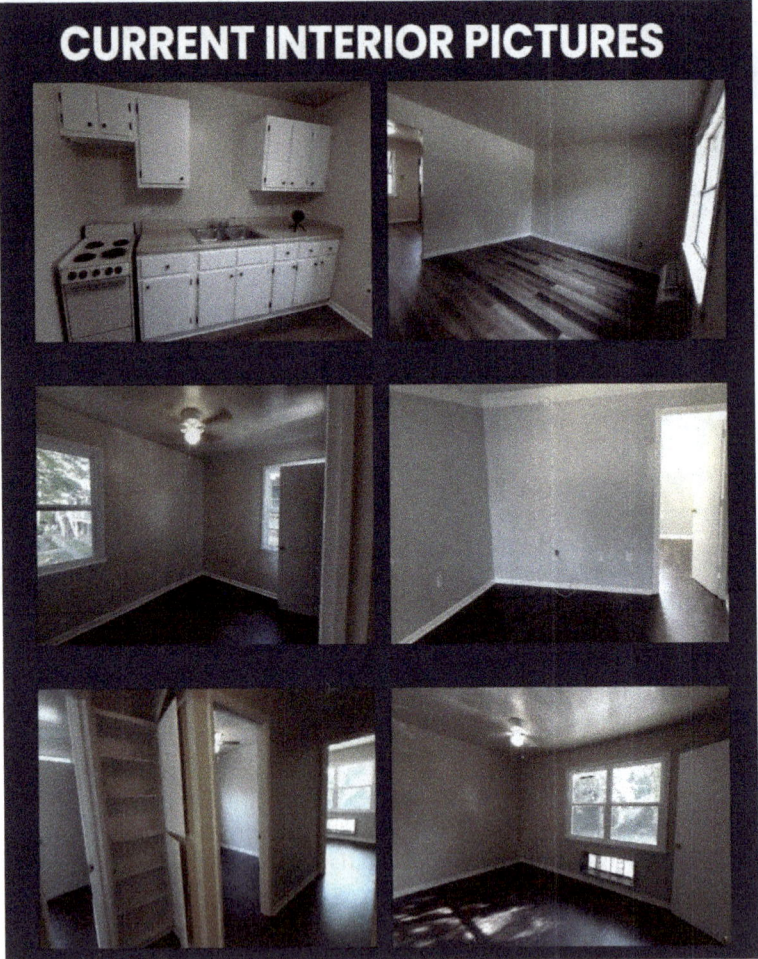

CURRENT INTERIOR PICTURES

The interior units are in great condition. They have been treated well by the tenants over the years. The previous owners did a great job with the renovations on the property, painting cabinets, installing new luxury vinyl plank flooring, and updating the bathrooms.

We call one of these different factors **The Horse** because it's all related to the property and the area of the property. Next, we are going to talk about **The Jockey**, who is the operator of the deal.

If you haven't yet. **You can grab yourself a copy of the Sample Deal Package here:**
https://www.reciprocitycg.com/sample-deal-package

Jockey – The Operator

We call the operators the Jockey. They are the ones with the horse, training, and operating, and they have the experience to turn a dud horse into a champion winner.

Mike's Perspective:

The Jockey can make or break a good deal. Unfortunately, I've seen a lot of good deals go bad over the last few years because the operators didn't have proper risk management. Not that they were being aggressive, but being new to the industry and inexperienced, they didn't ask the right questions.

One of the high-level masterminds I joined back in 2020 focused on multi-family investing. This mastermind costs $20,000 to join, so there's a high barrier to entry. I noticed back in 2020 that many new real estate investors were trying to get in. With interest rates so low, everyone was making money. Even those buying bad deals were making money because the market saved them with low interest rates, pushing up property values.

The nice thing about being in groups like this is that I get a real-time feel for how the market is going. I get a sense of the good, the bad, and the ugly. Well, in 2020, it was red-hot; interest rates for commercial real estate were in the low 3%s, and deals were getting done left and right. But when I saw people buying a deal and then, six months later, selling the same deal for a $1,000,000 profit, I knew something was off. It's like the famous quote goes:

"To be fearful when others are greedy and to be greedy only when others are fearful."

- Warren Buffett

It's very interesting how many potential deals I see that are either for sale or have sold. Many of these deals are sold with the "opportunity" to raise rents to market and hopefully make a decent return after rents are raised and operations are stabilized.

Unfortunately, for many investors, this takes time, patience, a great team, and experience, and if any one of these doesn't pan out, a turnaround project could fail.

We have run into one of these situations ourselves, where our property manager was missing the mark on raising rents and advertising units. We quickly realized the issues and implemented changes to the property management team. Since that change, our property has performed well, and we were able to refinance at a higher value.

Our company, Reciprocity Capital Group, has passed on literally thousands of deals that didn't make sense. There were many times we looked at each other, asking, ***"Are we the crazy ones?"*** How are so many people who are new to the industry finding so many great deals?

Thankfully, Adam and I stuck to our game plan and didn't let greed or fear of missing out get the best of us. Because now, when I see the same people four years later, a lot of their deals are going bad, and some even go into foreclosure.

I've asked hundreds of investors what's going on and what went wrong. There are three common mistakes they made. I'm going to share them with you.

1. **Variable Vs Fixed Rate Debt:** We always urge people to buy fixed-rate debt, even if it costs more money.

Why? Because it's predictable; every month, you know what your payment is going to be. Well, in 2020, when interest rates were super low and Jerome Powell, the head of the Federal Reserve, was going on T.V. saying they would not touch interest rates for four more years, investors felt comfortable taking the risk of buying a variable loan because it was maybe 0.5% - 1% cheaper than buying a fixed-rate loan.

When talking about millions of dollars in loans, that's substantial savings. They can then show their investors they expect higher returns and look like superheroes.

Well, all of that is fine and dandy if interest rates stay the same. But as we know, in 2022, rates started climbing, and by 2024, they are more than double what they were before. Now, their payments for the same property have drastically gone up, and some of the deals are not able to pay their debts.

Even though we heard the same message from the Federal Reserve, we have a healthy skepticism and love predictability. That's why all of our properties are bought on a fixed payment plan, and our deals are in a very healthy place.

2. **Overestimating Rent Increases:** Rents typically increase about 2-3% per year with a healthy and steady incline. But during 2020, when interest rates were low, inflation was high, and rent increases boomed. This can happen for a short period of time, and it's good not to believe this is the new normal.

Looking over some investors' deals, they were projecting that rents would continue to increase 15% per year for multiple years, making their returns look amazing! But in reality, they were being overly aggressive on the future rent increases.

3. **Renovation Costs:** If you aren't an experienced rehabber like I am, you wouldn't realize that the price of materials have doubled or even tripled since 2020. I was looking at the price of cabinets that we bought at Home Depot at the beginning of 2020; they were, on average about $145 per cabinet. Our team looked a few weeks ago, and the same exact cabinets are now $330 on average. That's a huge price difference.

Can you guess what else has significantly increased? The price of labor.

Now, making even a simple unit turn of paint and flooring is a lot more expensive than it has been in the past.

This is why it's very important to make sure the Jockey you are working with has realistic expectations of renovation costs for their project.

I've seen deals where the Jockey was expecting to do a full interior renovation with new luxury vinyl plank flooring, paint, cabinets, doors, trim, new toilet, vanity, and tub surround for $5,000 per unit.

Yikes.

$5,000 per unit nowadays is just some flooring and paint. A very light renovation.

We are seeing full interior renovations come in at about $15,000 per unit.

(Example of what a $15,000 unit renovation looks like)

Imagine being off on construction costs by $10,000 per unit, on a 100-unit apartment complex. That's an easy million-dollar mistake right there.

Like I said, none of these people are bad or have bad intentions. It's just the inexperience of being new in the real estate world and not having the proper risk management.

"It ain't what you don't know that gets you into trouble. It's what you know for sure that just ain't so."

— Mark Twain

Final Thoughts:

As you come to the end of this book, we want to give you a **big virtual high-five** for sticking with it! 👋 Seriously, there is a <u>TON</u> of information packed into this little book. Years and years of experience and knowledge are packed into here, and being successful takes a lot of commitment, and you've shown that in spades.

We hope you're feeling inspired by the potential of multi-family real estate. From learning about the benefits of passive income to understanding the power of diversification, you've gained some seriously valuable insights along the way.

But hey, learning is just the beginning. Real success in this game comes from putting that knowledge into action. It's about taking the leap and getting your money to work for you. Whether it's exploring investment opportunities, considering syndication deals, or even diversifying your portfolio, now's the time to turn those insights into action.

Adam and Mike are passionate about helping passive investors thrive in multi-family real estate. We'd be thrilled to continue this journey with you.

Got questions? Need some guidance on your next move? Or maybe you just want to chat about how you can take your passive investing to the next level? We're here for you. Seriously, we'd love to set up a 1-on-1 call and dive deeper into your goals and how we can help you achieve them.

Click here if you are on the digital version or enter the website link below to fill out a short questionnaire and book a 1-on-1 call with Mike and Adam. https://www.reciprocitycg.com/start-investing

Or scan the QR Code:

Before we sign off, we just want to say a huge thank you for choosing to invest your time with us and this book. Your commitment to growing your wealth as an investor is truly inspiring, and we can't wait to see where your journey in multi-family real estate takes you. Here's to your continued success and all the incredible opportunities waiting for you in the world of passive multi-family investing.

Adam Demchik and Mike Mannino II at Reciprocity Capital Group

END

Resources Page:

You can grab yourself a copy of the Sample Deal Package here: https://www.reciprocitycg.com/sample-deal-package

Click here if you are on the digital version or enter the website link below to fill out a short questionnaire and book a 1-on-1 call with Mike and Adam. https://www.reciprocitycg.com/start-investing

Or scan the QR Code:

If you would like to work with Mike 1-on-1 being an active investor click this link to book a call: https://www.rewbuilders.com/book-a-call

Legal Disclaimer:

The information provided in this book is for educational and informational purposes only. While the author has made every effort to ensure the accuracy and completeness of the content, they are not providing legal, accounting, tax, or investment advice.

Readers are advised to consult with their own qualified professionals, including but not limited to accountants, tax advisors, and attorneys, before making any financial or investment decisions based on the information presented in this book.

The strategies, techniques, and concepts discussed in this book, including but not limited to depreciation, 1031 exchanges, and tax benefits associated with holding multi-family properties, may have legal, tax, or financial implications that vary based on individual circumstances and jurisdictional requirements.

The author and publisher disclaim any liability or responsibility for any loss or damage resulting from reliance on the information provided in this book.

Readers should independently verify any information contained herein and seek professional advice tailored to their specific situation before implementing any strategies or making any investment decisions.

By reading this book, you acknowledge and agree that the author is not providing personalized financial, tax, or legal advice and that you are solely responsible for evaluating and determining the suitability of any strategies or recommendations for your own financial and investment objectives.

This document is for educational purposes only and does not constitute an offer to purchase or sell securitized real estate investments. Private Real Estate Investments are available to accredited investors and accredited entities only. Requirements for accreditation are defined in Rule 501 of Regulation D. Investors are required to self-certify their accreditation status and should consult a CPA or attorney if uncertain.

There are risks associated with investing in multi-family real estate, including, but not limited to, loss of entire investment principal, declining market values, tenant vacancies, and illiquidity. Potential cash flows, returns, and asset appreciation are not guaranteed and could be lower than anticipated. Past performance is not indicative of future returns.

Individual investor needs and objectives vary, and this document is not intended to indicate multi-family suitability for any particular investor. In addition, it should not be interpreted as tax or legal advice. Investors considering a multi-family investment should speak with their tax and legal advisors for advice and/or guidance regarding their individual financial situation.

Photos in this document are either original or open-sourced. They are for illustrative purposes only and do not represent current or future multi-family offerings.